Bond
No.1 for exam success

No Nonsense
English

9–10 years

OXFORD
UNIVERSITY PRESS

D0491749

Contents

Copy this piece of writing on the lines underneath.

How to make a pobble cake
First get three large plibs. Clean the skins and dry
them. Then beat up two eggs, add a pinch of salt and
mix together. Roll the plibs in the mixture. Get a
large board and two handfuls of best pobble. Roll
the pobble out on the board until it is quite thin. Put
it in a frying pan. Pour the plibs and eggs on top.
Throw the whole mixture in the air three or four
times. Bake in a hot oven and serve with slug sauce.

Copy this poem on the lines underneath. You might like to try making your writing slope forward a bit.

I don't like Mondays. I really don't. It's my worst day of the week by far. First I have to get up an extra fifteen minutes early because my Mum starts work earlier. That means I walk to school at the same time as Bully Watson. Bully Watson's a terror – he's built like a barn door and if he grabs you by the ear you don't half feel it. If you dodge him there's always a chance you'll meet The Dog. It's a snarling beast with huge fangs. I'm sure it's an escaped wolf.

Vowel endings

> Many nouns that end with a vowel end in **e**:
>   tun**e**
> Some nouns end with **a i o** or **u**:
>   camer**a**   scamp**i**   her**o**   gn**u**

1. **Use a vowel to complete these nouns to do with food and music.**

   a banj__   **b** pizz__   **c** risott__   **d** raviol__   **e** banan__   **f** concert__

   g cell__   **h** past__   **i** viol__   **j** pian__   **k** disc__   **l** bong__

2. **Write the names of the animals described. They all end with a vowel.**

   a A striped animal with hooves that lives in Africa.   z_____

   b An Australian animal that keeps its young in a pouch.   k_____

   c A dangerous, hooded snake that lives in Africa and India. c_____

> To change a word ending in a vowel from singular to plural follow these rules.
> If the noun ends in:
> • **one vowel** add **s** or **es**   camer**a** / camera**s**   her**o** / hero**es**
> It's hard sometimes to know if the plural is **s** or **es**!
> • **two vowels** add **s**   tatt**oo** / tattoo**s**
>
> QUICK TIP!
> The singular and plural of some words are the same.

3. **Write the plural of these words.**

   a igloo _____   **b** piano _____   **c** echo _____

   d cargo _____   **e** mango _____   **f** case _____

4. **Complete the sentences by changing the nouns in brackets to plurals.**

   a Mum put _____ and _____ in the salad.
   (tomato / avocado)

   b The cowboys swirled their _____ around their heads. (lasso)

   c Mum uses _____ to make chips. (potato)

0			24
Tough	OK	Got it!	

Total
/24

Plurals

Most plurals end in s: newspaper**s**   dog**s**   pet**s**
But if the noun ends in **ch, sh, x, s** or **ss** add **es**:
    wat**ch** / watch**es** fo**x** / fox**es**

> **QUICK TIP!**
> **Singular** means one, **plural** means more than one.

1. Write the plural of these singular nouns.

a leach _____   **b** wish _____   **c** gas _____

d box _____   **e** supper _____   **f** fork _____

2. Write the singular of these plural nouns.

a dishes _____   **b** lunches _____   **c** books _____

d brushes _____   **e** faxes _____   **f** classes _____

If the noun ends in:
- a **vowel** and **y** add **s**   vall**ey** / valley**s**
- a **consonant** and **y** delete the y and add **ies**   ba**by** / bab**ies**
- **f** or **fe** usually delete the f or fe and add **ves**   loa**f** / loa**ves**   kni**fe** / kni**ves**

3. Write the plural of these singular nouns.

a berry _____   **b** city _____   **c** cross _____

d leaf _____   **e** toy _____   **f** wife _____

4. Write the singular of these plural nouns.

a jellies _____   **b** halves _____   **c** poppies _____

d lives _____   **e** trays _____   **f** wolves _____

5. Complete these sentences using the plural of the word in brackets.

a The cow had two new-born _____ nuzzling against her. (calf)

b Grandpa and Grandma are both in their _____ . (seventy)

c She used lots of sweet _____ to make a shiny birthday card. (wrapper)

0			27
Tough	OK	Got it!	

Total

/27

5

Prefixes 1

> Knowing the spelling and meaning of a prefix can help with the spelling and meaning of a new word.
>
> **auto** means **self**   **bi** means **two**   **circum** means **around**
> **tele** means **distant**   **trans** means **across**

1. **Add bi or tele to the words below and write them next to their meanings.**

   scope   vision   lingual   focals   cycle

   a Spectacles with two uses: helping you see things close-up and far away. _____

   b A machine with which you can see moving pictures and hear sound. _____

   c Someone who can speak two languages fluently. _____

   d A tube you look through to see distant objects more clearly. _____

   e A means of transport with two wheels. _____

2. **Use auto, circum or trans to complete these words.**

   a _____matic   **b** _____vent   **c** _____navigate

   d _____form   **e** _____scribe   **f** _____port

   g _____psy   **h** _____plant   **i** _____mit

   > **QUICK TIP!**
   > **Circum** sometimes shortens to **circ** or **circu** before letters such as **l** or **s**.

3. **Complete the words in these sentences using one of these prefixes.**

   auto   bi   circum   tele   trans

   a A _____plane was an early type of aeroplane with two sets of wings.

   b Some people like to collect _____graphs of celebrities.

   c Lorna can _____late English words into French words.

   d Many famous people write their _____biography.

   e My dad likes to watch sport on _____vision.

   f His arms were very strong. His _____ceps were very muscular.

   g She measured the _____ference of the larger circle.

0			21
Tough	OK	Got it!	

Total

/ 21

Synonyms

Words that have similar meanings are called **synonyms**. They make writing more interesting to read.

He **went** to the door.   He **hobbled** to the door.

The word 'went' doesn't tell us very much but 'hobbled' puts a picture in our minds. The chosen synonym must fit the **context** of a sentence.

It was a **bright** and sunny day. ✓

It was a **shiny** and sunny day. ✗

1. **Match these synonyms with their meanings.**

   a anger   to cause distress or overturn something

   b irritate   to make someone very cross

   c prevent   to annoy someone

   d upset   to stop someone from doing something

   > QUICK TIP!
   > Use a thesaurus to find synonyms.

2. **Complete the groups of synonyms in the table, using these words.**   *(12 marks)*

   giggle strike sticker rap ticket chuckle badge guffaw bang chortle swipe tag

knock				
label				
laugh				

3. **Choose the most appropriate synonym to complete the sentences.**

   a The child made such a _____ when it was time to leave. (site / scene)

   b The student was punished for _____ his friend's notes. (copying / imitating)

   c Dad was _____ when I erased the rugby match he recorded. (insane / angry)

4. **Put these synonyms in order from the least to the most. Use a dictionary to help!**

   a ravenous / hungry / peckish _____ _____ _____

   b terrified / alarmed / startled _____ _____ _____

   c trot / gallop / walk / canter _____ _____ _____ _____

0	Tough	OK	Got it!	22

Total

/22

Adverbs

> Putting an **adverb** with the verb after someone has said something tells us more about the way in which it was said.
>
> "Do I have to get up now?" Stephen murmured **sleepily**.
>
>   ↑   ↑
>
>   verb   adverb

1. **Underline the adverbs in these phrases.**

    a he sighed wearily   **b** she replied politely   **c** he breathed noisily

    d loudly they cheered   **e** we shouted joyfully   **f** anxiously they whispered

2. **What is identical in the spelling of these adverbs?**

    _____

    _____

> **QUICK TIP!**
> Remember what happens to **y** when you add a suffix.

3. **Turn these adjectives into adverbs.**

    a triumphant _____   **b** happy _____   **c** quiet _____

    d nasty _____   **e** calm _____   **f** cheerful _____

4. **Complete these phrases using the most appropriate adverb.**

    silently   noisily   angrily   wearily   excitedly   politely

    a sighed _____   **b** replied _____   **c** snored _____

    d cheered _____   **e** prayed _____   **f** shouted _____

5. **Change the adjectives into adverbs and complete each sentence.**

    a "Can we really stay a bit longer?" cried Simon _____. (excited)

    b "Get off my land!" shouted the farmer _____. (furious)

    c "It's no good. No matter how hard I try, I never win," Jo replied _____. (gloomy)

    d "Of course I know him," Abid replied _____, "he's my brother!" (proud)

    e "I'm sorry you're moving away," whispered Carol _____. (sad)

			Total
0		24	
Tough	OK	Got it!	/24

Root words

Many words are developed from a base or root word.
- **sign** comes from Latin and means a sign, an emblem
- **take** means to grasp, to get possession of
- **phone** is to do with sound
- **bomb** comes from Latin and means a booming sound

> QUICK TIP!
> Use the spelling of the root word to help spell the new word.

1. Match these words to their meanings.   *(4 marks)*

overtake	to get something wrong	include	keep out or leave out
partake	to catch up and get past	exclude	hide from view, keep away
mistake	to get a share in	seclude	add, join in, be part of
bomb	soldiers with heavy weapons	phone	not genuine, not real
bombastic	highly explosive materials	phoneme	a telephone
bombardiers	pompous speech or writing	phoney	a speech sound

2. Add sign to these words to make other words and look up their meanings.

a _ _ _ _ al = _____   it means _____

b _ _ _ _ ature = _____   it means _____

c re_ _ _ _ ed = _____   it means _____

d de_ _ _ _ = _____   it means _____

e in_ _ _ _ ificant = _____   it means _____

3. Complete each sentence using a word that includes the root word given in brackets.

a The shop _____ helped her find the right size dress. (assist)

b The Prime Minister is the leader of the _____. (govern)

c The thief was _____ for three years. (prison)

d Liz is my aunt and Sam is another _____. (relate)

e The archaeologist made a fascinating _____ at the dig. (cover)

f "Please, _____ me. I'm really sorry for what I did." (give)

| 0 | | | 15 |
| Tough | OK | Got it! | |

Total

/15

Changing word order

Changing the word order in a sentence does not always change the meaning.
   Jim raced after the **horse** last week. Last week **Jim** raced after the **horse**.
The second sentence **means the same** as the first but is more powerful.
If you exchange the subject and the object the **meaning changes**.
   The **horse** chased after **Jim** last week.

1. **Change these sentences around to make them stronger, more exciting.**

   a No one was there when she opened the door.

   _____

   b The birds flew away with a flurry of wings.

   _____

   c A red squirrel scrambled up the tree.

   _____

2. **Switch the subject and object in these sentences to change the meaning.**

   a The man startled the rabbit.

   _____

   b The horse raced after Jim.

   _____

   c Raj beat Carole in the 100 metre sprint.

   _____

3. **Write a sentence of your own with a subject and an object.**

   a _____

   Change the word order but not the meaning.

   b _____

   Exchange the subject and the object to change the meaning.

   c _____

			Total
0 Tough	OK	Got it! 9	9

Editing text

After you have written a piece of work you need to read it through and **edit** it to check:
- that **meanings** are clear
- that **spelling**, **punctuation** and **grammar** are correct
- if any sentences can be improved by using different **connectives** or by **deleting unnecessary words**.

1. **Choose connectives to join these sentences. Avoid using 'because' or 'but'.**

   a I missed the bus. I walked home.

   I missed the bus, so I walked home.

   b I took my umbrella. It was pouring with rain.

   _____

   c We went by car. We could have walked home.

   _____

   d We couldn't visit Katie. She was ill. We went to the pictures instead.

   _____

2. **Cross out the unnecessary words in these sentences. Rewrite each sentence using ten words or less.**

   a The ~~big, huge,~~ enormous elephant was moving ~~large,~~ heavy ~~pieces of~~ tree trunk.

   The enormous elephant was moving heavy tree trunks.

   b The baby's round, chubby face was covered all over with messy, gooey chocolate.

   _____

   c Kay whispered very quietly in Lee's ear, "We should get out from here, now!"

   _____

   d Bev packed her sandals, swimming costume and lots of other clothes for her holiday.

   _____

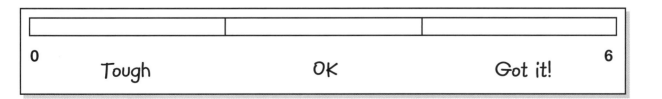

Tough	OK	Got it!

0   6

Total

/6

Speech

There are two types of written speech: **direct** speech and **reported** speech.

Direct speech means writing what a character actually says:
  "Let's go to see Fred," suggested Kamal.

Reported speech means writing that a character said something:
  Kamal suggested that we went to see Fred.

QUICK TIP!
Direct speech needs speech marks; reported speech doesn't.

1. **Rewrite these sentences with direct speech in place of the reported speech.**

   a Mum said that she couldn't come to the concert because she was working.

   Mum said, "I can't come

   b The lady asked Dinah if she had forgotten her bus fare.

   _____

   c Harry asked Priti if she wanted to go swimming.

   _____

   d Mum told Belinda that she had to hurry up or she would be late.

   _____

2. **Rewrite these sentences with reported speech in place of the direct speech.**

   a "Good morning, Mr Smith, and how are you feeling?" asked the nurse.

   The nurse said good morning

   b "Don't forget to brush your teeth before you go to bed," Dad reminded me.

   _____

   c "Shh! Try to be quieter, or you'll wake the baby," Mum whispered to me.

   _____

   d "No scribble today," the teacher said. "I only want to see your best writing."

   _____

0			8
Tough	OK	Got it!	

Total

/8

Auxiliary verbs

Some verbs need a helping verb, known as an **auxiliary verb**:
   I **have given** my brother a present. 'have' is the auxiliary verb and 'given' is the main verb.

Auxiliary verbs help to form the **tense** of the sentence.
Some common forms of auxiliary verbs are:
   be   being   been   has   had   have   do   did

Others include:
   am   is   are   can   could   was   were   might   will   should   would

There can be **more than one** auxiliary verb helping the main verb.
   "I **have been** playing with my brother."

1. **Underline the auxiliary verbs in these sentences.**

   a The train arrived earlier than we had expected.

   b I will wait for Sylvan to come home, as he should be here soon.

   c He said that he could do it straight away.

   d She told me that she might visit tomorrow but we are going to be out.

2. **Change the sentences into the present tense by changing the auxiliary verb.**

   a They were carrying the picnic box. _____

   b We were waiting for the bus. _____

   c He was cycling around the garden. _____

   d I was eating my breakfast. _____

3. **Change the sentences into the past tense by changing the auxiliary verb.**

   a Claire is doing the washing up. _____

   b We have leading roles in the play. _____

   c The roadworks are finished. _____

   d I will be painting a picture. _____

0		12
Tough	OK	Got it!

Total

12

First, second and third person

When you write about something, you can use **different points of view**. When you write from your own point of view, this is called writing in the **first person**.

	Singular	Plural
First person – talking about myself used for diaries, personal letters	I	we
Second person – talking to someone else used for instructions and directions	you	you
Third person – talking to another person about someone else used for narrative and recounts	he / she / it	they

1. **Fill in the gaps using the correct personal pronoun, indicated in brackets.**

   a _____ buy all their vegetables at the farm shop. (third person plural)

   b _____ always eats her vegetables. (third person singular)

   c _____ went to the cricket match on Saturday. (first person singular)

   d "Are _____ waiting for a bus to Lewisham?" (second person singular)

2. **Write these sentences in the third person.**

   a We went to see Laura today. _They_____

   b I am running in the race. _____

   c We chased the cat away. _____

   d I live in an apartment. _____

3. **Write these sentences in the second person.**

   a Did he play tennis last week? _Did you_____

   b They will stay at home today. _____

   c He is nearly as tall as his father. _____

   d She planted a new lawn. _____

0	Tough	OK	Got it!	12

Total

/12

Commas and clauses 1

In a **complex sentence**, there is a **main clause** (key information) and a **subordinate clause** (extra information).

When the subordinate clause begins a sentence, a **comma** is needed between it and the main clause.

Although he was late, Ian didn't hurry.

The subordinate clause doesn't make sense by itself.

The main clause makes sense by itself.

1. **Write the missing comma in each of these sentences.**

   a After it raced along the tarmac the plane took off.

   b Although the skin was bitter the flesh of the fruit was sweet.

   c As the noise in the tunnel grew louder the children screamed.

   d So that she could see some lions Amy went on safari.

2. **Join the clauses then write the full sentences with commas.**

   Although Brian shouldn't have   Ranjit went to the garage.
   Even though she didn't want to   I escape to my bedroom.
   To get a spanner   he decided to go.
   When I want to be alone   Erin helped her Mum.

   a _____

   b _____

   c _____

   d _____

3. **Tick the sentences with a comma in the correct place. Correct the ones that are incorrect.**

   a As I get older, I grow taller.

   b So, he wouldn't be late Ian ran quickly.

   c If it isn't, too cold we'll play on the swings.

   d Although I'd like to, I can't join in because I've hurt my ankle.

0			12
Tough	OK	Got it!	

Total

/12

Colons, semicolons, hyphens and dashes

Colons introduce lists or examples.

Semicolons join together two complete sentences and separate items in detailed lists:

They visited three capital cities: Paris, France; London, England; and Tokyo, Japan.

Hyphens are sometimes used to join two parts of compound words. They are also used in between some prefixes and root words: ex-teacher, self-centred.

Dashes are an informal type of punctuation and indicate a pause:
He watched carefully – nothing moved.

1. **Write the missing colons and semicolons in these sentences.**

   a Here are the directions leave the M3 at Junction 1 and turn left on to the A308.

   b The presents I still need to buy are a CD for Ying a book token for Gran and earrings for Mum.

   c Some boys are great footballers others are not.

   d Shakespeare wrote "To be or not to be."

2. **Write the missing hyphens in these sentences.**

   a She painted twenty one self portraits.

   b The question showed a three dimensional cube.

   c "Mum, can I have a jack in the box for my birthday please?"

   d He had to re sort the playing cards into their suits before playing the game.

3. **Write the missing dashes in these sentences.**

   a The ice cream had melted the fridge had broken down.

   b There's no sound from the dryer it must have finished.

   c I live in that house the one with the green door.

   d The sky had clouded over a splatter of rain could be seen on the window.

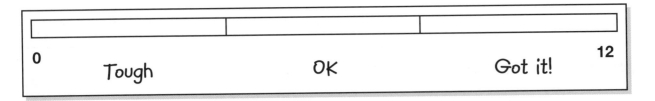

			Total
0			12
Tough	OK	Got it!	

12

Dialogue

When characters in a story talk to each other, it is called **dialogue**.

Speech marks go around the dialogue to show when someone is speaking.

A **comma** is used to separate the speech from the narrative.

When a **different character** speaks, their speech is written on a **new line**.
"Morning Miss," said the pupils.
"Good morning, Year 5," replied the teacher.

1. **Put the correct punctuation and speech marks into these sentences.**

   a Don't do that said the teacher It's dangerous

   b Wait he yelled Come back here

   c It's not fair I didn't do anything she wailed

   d The boy teetered on the edge of the cliff Lee she shouted Don't move

2. **Rewrite this passage adding the correct speech punctuation, including new lines for new speakers.**   (8 marks)

   You'll never do it said Josh. You want to bet asked Angela. Go on then he laughed see if you can climb that tree I don't think you will. But she did climb the tree and threw the Frisbee back down. There you are she said I told you I could do it. Yes you did tell me but I didn't think you would he said looking sheepish. Oh well she said at least we got our Frisbee back.

   _____

   _____

   _____

   _____

   _____

   _____

   _____

			Total
0 Tough	OK	Got it! 12	/12

Story openings

A good story must have a good **opening**. There are several common features to a good opening:
- It must grab the reader's attention from the very start.

Read the start of this story and answer the questions.

"All aboard?" said the captain.
"All aboard, sir!" said the mate.
"Then stand by to let her go."

1. **Where is the story set and what is about to happen?**

_____

2. **Does this opening grab your attention? Can you say why?**

_____

- The writer must quickly give details of when and where the story is set.

Read the next part of the story and answer the questions.

It was nine o'clock on a Wednesday morning. The good ship *Spartan* was lying off Boston Quay with everything prepared for a start. The final bell had been rung. Her bowsprit was turned towards England. The hiss of escaping steam showed that all was ready for her run of three thousand miles. She strained at the ropes that held her like a greyhound at its leash.

3. **Where and exactly when is this part of the story set?**

_____

4. **Where is the *Spartan* going and how long is the journey?**

_____

5. **What kind of ship is the *Spartan*? Which phrase tells you how it is powered?**

_____

6. **What is the ship compared to in this part of the story?**

_____

- The opening must introduce one or more characters.

- It must also quickly introduce some problem or threat that will develop the story in an interesting way.

- It needs to use interesting language to set the scene.

Here is the third part of the opening of this story.

I have the misfortune of being a very nervous man. As I stood upon the quarter-deck of the Transatlantic steamer, I bitterly cursed the necessity which drove me back to the land of my fathers. The shouts of the sailors, the rattle of the cordage, the farewells of my fellow-passengers, and the cheers of the crowd, all disturbed me.

I felt sad too. An indescribable feeling, as of some impending calamity, seemed to haunt me. The sea was calm, and the breeze light. Yet I felt as if I stood upon the verge of a great danger. Had I known the experience which awaited me in the course of the next twelve hours I would, even then, at the last moment have sprung upon the shore, and made my escape from the cursed vessel.

7. **What is the hero of the story like and how does he feel?**

8. **Why was it not reasonable for him to feel worried as the ship left?**

9. **What phrases near the end suggest that something terrible is about to happen?**

10. **Would this opening make you want to read on? Can you say why?**

0			10
Tough	OK	Got it!	

Total

/ 10

Recount writing

Recounts retell past events and focus on specific people or incidents. Recounts may be either **personal**, such as a report of a school trip, or **impersonal**, such as a newspaper report. All good recounts are written in the past tense and have:

- an **introduction** – to give an overview of the event
- a series of events detailed in **chronological** order
- an organised **structure**, using paragraphs
- the use of **time connectives**, such as: after, next, meanwhile, then
- the use of **technical language** relevant to the topic
- a **closing statement** that comments on or evaluates the events.

Read this recount and answer the questions.

I woke up early on Saturday as it was my birthday and Mum and Dad were taking me on a surprise birthday trip! They were taking me to the safari park and I was really excited as I had never been there before.

First, we saw the giraffe and zebra paddock, but we carried on as they weren't very interesting. Next were the flamingos, which were weird. They were all standing on one leg with their heads upside down in the water.

After that, we moved on into the monkey enclosure where there was plenty of action! There were loads of monkeys and they were jumping all over the cars. One large monkey jumped onto our car and started pulling at the aerial. We all thought it was funny – until he ran off with it. Dad was furious!

Lastly, we saw the lions. I learned that they are carnivores – meat eaters. They feed on herbivores, such as giraffe and zebra, so it's a good thing the animals are kept apart. The lions are meant to be very dangerous but they looked very lazy to me. They were all lying down sunbathing!

When we had seen all the wild animals, we stopped in the picnic area for lunch. Then we went to see the animals in 'pets corner' before going home. It was a brilliant day and I think it was the best surprise birthday trip I have ever had.

1. **What is a safari park? Circle the correct answer.**

   an amusement park   a large wildlife area   a museum

2. **How many paragraphs make up this recount? Which one gives an overview of the events?**

   _____

3. How many time connectives does the writer include? List them all.

_____

4. List any technical terms you found in the recount.

_____

5. Is this a personal or impersonal recount? How can you tell?

_____

_____

6. Does the writer evaluate the events? If so, where?

_____

_____

7. Retell the recount in your own words in five short sentences.

a Introduction _____

_____

b First _____

_____

c Next _____

_____

d Finally _____

_____

e Evaluation _____

_____

0 Tough   OK   Got it!   **11**

Total

11

How am I doing?

1. **Write the plurals for these nouns.**

   a domino _____   **b** safari _____   **c** bench _____

   d potato _____   **e** pony _____   **f** loss _____

2. **Choose a prefix from auto, bi, circum, tele or trans to complete these words.**

   a _____matic   **b** _____vent   **c** _____form   **d** _____plant

   e _____stance   **f** _____pilot   **g** _____vise   **h** _____pathy

3. **Write these synonyms in order from the least to the most.**

   a sob / wail / cry   _____ _____ _____

   b scream / whisper / shout   _____ _____ _____

   c amused / delirious / happy   _____ _____ _____

4. **Complete these phrases using the most appropriate adverb.**

   quietly   enthusiastically   loudly   sweetly   tentatively   calmly

   a She sang _____   **b** He whispered _____   **c** They whooped _____

   d I replied _____   **e** Mum shouted _____   **f** Jim asked _____

5. **Write down the root word shared by the pairs of words.**

   a signal / signature _____   **b** bombard / bombastic _____

   c imbalance / unbalanced _____   **d** publicity / publications _____

6. **Change the word order, but not the meaning, of these sentences.**

   a We visited Grandma on Monday. _____

   b For dinner, Mum cooked some fish. _____

7. **Write these sentences of reported speech as direct speech.**

   a John asked her if she wanted a cup of tea.

   _____

   b The teacher said that Suki was ill and would not be in school today.

   _____

8. **Write these sentences in the past tense by changing the auxiliary verb.**

   a The bus is arriving early. _____

   b I am waiting for Oscar. _____

   c Dad is going to cook dinner. _____

9. **Complete these sentences in the third person.**

   a _____ went to visit their Grandpa last week.

   b _____ was riding his bike around the garden.

   c I sat on the chair and _____ snapped in two!

10. **Underline the subordinate clauses and separate them from the main clauses with commas.**

   a As it is so hot today I would like an ice cream.

   b Although it was raining we decided to go shopping.

   c I saw a kite which was red and yellow tangled in a tree.

11. **Write in the missing colons, semicolons, hyphens or dashes.**

   a Inside the package was a scarf a packet of biscuits from Gran and a letter from Mum.

   b Please can we go there I promise to be good.

   c Wordsworth wrote "Our souls have sight of that immortal sea".

12. **Rewrite this exchange of dialogue correctly.**   *(4 marks)*

   where shall we go karisma asked i don't mind replied sophie anywhere you like i think i'd like to go to the park so we can play on the see-saw karisma answered

   _____

   _____

   _____

   _____

Total

47

Hard and soft c

> When the letter **c** is followed by **e**, **i** or **y** it usually gives a **soft**, hissing sound: **c**eiling.
> When it is followed by **a**, **o** or **u** it is usually a **hard k** sound: **c**ot.

1. **Circle the words that have a soft c sound and underline those with a hard c sound.**

   cinema   cord   camel   celery   caught   certain

   card   decimal lacy   culinary cereal   curtain $\left(\frac{1}{2}\ mark\ for\ each\right)$

2. **Circle the words with soft or hard c sounds in these sentences, then list them in the table.**

	soft c	hard c
a Jay had to recite a poem at the concert.		
b Carl and Jim went to the ceremony.		
c He cut a circle from the piece of wood.		
d Susie made lots of Christmas cards.		

> QUICK TIP!
> A word can contain both a soft and a hard c: circus!

3. **Underline the misspelt words and write the correct spellings.**

   a We went to the sinema last Saturday. _____

   b Dad took us to see Koventry Sity play. _____

   c Going for a walk every day is good for your sirkulation. _____

   d Riding a bisykle is good exersise. _____

   e Saris are very colourful klothes. _____

   f Sally is going to the karnival in Desember. _____

   g She kouldn't deside which jumper to wear. _____

			Total
0		17	
Tough	OK	Got it!	

/17

Common letter strings

Some letter strings are **pronounced** differently in different words. Here are the most common pronunciations of **ough**, **ou**, **oo** and **our**:

Sounds like	ough	ou	oo	our
oh	though	boulder		
ow	bough	found		flour
uh	borough	young		armour
aw	ought			pour
oo	through	group	mood	
short oo		should	good	

> QUICK TIP!
> **ough** can also sound like **uff** (**tough**) and **off** (**cough**).

1. **Group these words together by their pronunciation.**   (*18 marks*)

   ghoul   couple   bouquet   yours   plough   mourn   could   hood
   bamboo   soul   favour   cook   hour   shout   thorough   sought   although   cartoon

oh	ow	uh	aw	oo	short oo

2. **Complete the words with the correct spellings of the sounds in brackets.**

   a I am having s_____p ('oo') followed by chocolate m_____e ('oo') for lunch.

   b It t_____k (short 'oo') a break_____h ('oo') in science to find a cure.

   c She br_____t ('aw') some f_____d ('oo') but the cheese was m_____y. ('oh')

3. **Change or add one letter each time to make word ladders.**

   a cough   **b** book   **c** ear
   _rough_____   _____   _____
   _bough_____   _____   _____
   _bought_____   _____   _____
   _brought_____   _____   _____

0	Tough	OK	Got it!	23

Total

/23

Homophones

The word **homo** means same and **phone** means sound.
Homophones are words that **sound the same** but they are **spelt differently** and have **different meanings**:

    right / write   stare / stair   brake / break

1. **Link the sets of three homophones below.**   *(8 marks)*

rein	buy	reign		you	they're	sent
road	rain	sow		to	yew	there
by	so	rowed		their	scent	too
sew	rode	bye		cent	two	ewe

2. **Write a homophone for these words.**

  a beech _____   **b** grate _____   **c** know _____   **d** maid _____

  e mane _____   **f** pain _____   **g** scene _____   **h** waist _____

  i flour _____   **j** cell _____   **k** hymn _____   **l** here _____

3. **Select the correct homophone to complete these sentences.**

  a There are lots of _____ in Richmond Park. (dear / deer)

  b He kicked the ball straight _____ the window. (through / threw)

  c We were not _____ to climb the giant elm tree. (allowed / aloud)

  d A _____ carries your blood back to your heart. (vain / vein)

  e We all wanted a _____ of Charlie's birthday cake. (peace / piece)

4. **Think of a pair of homophones to answer these riddles.**

  a What opens locks and is also found in harbours? _____ / _____

  b What vegetable also describes a dripping tap? _____ / _____

  c What is on your head and an animal that lives in fields? _____ / _____

0			28
Tough	OK	Got it!	

Total

/28

Possessive pronouns

> **Possessive pronouns** show who **owns** something:
>   **mine / yours / his / hers / its / theirs / ours**   That book is **mine**.
>
> These possessive pronouns are used with nouns:
>   **my / your / his / her / its / their / our**   That is **my** book.

1. **Complete this chart by adding in the missing possessive pronouns.** ($\frac{1}{2}$ *mark for each*)

	Personal pronouns	Possessive pronouns used alone	Possessive pronouns used with nouns
First person singular	I		
Second person singular	you		
Third person singular	he / she / it		
First person plural	we		
Second person plural	you		
Third person plural	they		

2. **Underline the possessive pronouns in these sentences.**

    a Ali and Carrie walked to their home where their Mum was waiting for them.

    b "Please hand in your homework," said his teacher. "Is that yours, Ashley?"

    c The dog wagged its tail. "I'm glad he's ours," whispered Hailey.

    d Little Tommy had a go on our computer and he really messed up my work!

3. **Complete these sentences using possessive pronouns.**

    a The snake shed _____ skin.

    b "Is this _____ jacket and scarf?" the teacher asked Julie.

    c He gave me a ride on the back of _____ bike.

    d Our baby sister gets food all over _____ hands and face.

    e The elephant lifted _____ trunk and trumpeted very loudly.

    f Do you like _____ new dress that I bought for you yesterday?

0			16
Tough	OK	Got it!	

Total

16

Suffixes

> Several different suffixes make the sound **shun**.
> * **tion** – the **most common** ending: educate / educa**tion**
> * **ssion** – a **clear, soft 'sh'** sound: discuss / discu**ssion**
> * **cian** – common in **occupations**: music / musi**cian**
> * **sion** – when the root word ends in **d/de** or **s/se**: confuse / confu**sion**
> When a word ends in **d/de** or **s/se** remove those letters and add **sion**.

1. **Write these words with the correct suffix.**

   a explode _____   **b** transfuse _____

   c promote _____   **d** electric _____

   e direct _____   **f** politic _____

   g connect _____   **h** complete _____

   i discuss _____   **j** magic _____

2. **Choose the correct suffixes for these words.**

   a Two cars were involved in the _____. (collide)

   b I went to have my eyesight checked by an _____. (optic)

   c Someone who finds out what is wrong with you is a _____. (physic)

   d We took enough _____ for our journey. (provide)

   e Clothes in a sale are given a price _____. (reduce)

   f Things that belong to you are your _____. (possess)

   g "I have given Johnny _____ to watch _____." (permit / televise)

   h The flowers were a _____ of his _____. (demonstrate / devote)

3. **Tick the words with the correct suffix. Write the correct spelling of the ones that are wrong.**

   a electritian _____   **b** extension _____

   c decission _____   **d** permician _____

0			22
Tough	OK	Got it!	

Total

22

Onomatopoeia

Words like **bang**, **boom** and **whoosh** are examples of onomatopoeic words.
They **sound like** the **noise they describe**.

These words are very powerful and are often used in comics, poems and nursery rhymes.
They help readers to imagine a scene more clearly.

1. **Circle the onomatopoeic words.** ($\frac{1}{2}$ *mark for each*)

    wag   twitter   eat   miaow   stop   growl   croak

    ask   tweet   yelp   hoot   crunch   woof   splash

2. **Match each word with its meaning.**

    a buzz   The noise when something heavy falls on the floor.

    b slurp   The sound a bee makes when it flies.

    c thud   The sound of someone eating soup messily.

3. **Complete the sentences using these words.** ($\frac{1}{2}$ *mark for each*)

    sizzled   hiss   popped   whizzed   splattered   fizzed   fizzled   slithered

    a He heard the _____ of the snake as it _____ towards him.

    b The fireworks _____ up in the air then _____ out on the ground.

    c The sausages _____ in the frying pan and _____ the cooker's surface.

    d He _____ the can, poured the drink and it _____ in the glass.

4. **Replace the verb in the brackets with a more powerful onomatopoeic word.**

    a A timer _____ to show the food in the microwave was cooked. (rang)

    b Their boots _____ along the muddy streets. (slid)

    c The little piglets _____ when she picked them up. (cried)

    d The ducks _____ loudly at the farmer. (cried)

			Total
0			16
Tough	OK	Got it!	

16

29

Grammatical agreement

In a sentence, nouns and pronouns must always agree with the verb. The verb ending changes according to whether the noun/pronoun is singular or plural:

the girl dance   ✗   the girls dances   ✗
the girl **dances**   ✓   the girls **dance**   ✓

1. **Complete each pair of phrases using the correct form of the verb given.**

    a swing / swings   **b** cough / coughs   **c** sing / sings

    the monkey _____   the lady _____   the birds _____

    the monkeys _____   the ladies _____   the bird _____

2. **Circle the correct form of the verb in these sentences.**

    a Jed **uses** / **use** the computer every day.

    b Gran and Grandpa **live** / **lives** ten miles away.

    c People **cross** / **crosses** the road at the pedestrian crossing.

    d Oranges **grow** / **grows** in warm countries.

    e The dustman **empty** / **empties** the rubbish bins every Friday.

    f She asked Josh, "**Does** / **Do** we have to go home now?"

    g The dog **chew** / **chews** the bone.

3. **Complete the sentences using the correct form of the verb given in brackets.**

    a He always _____ to the shop. (to walk)

    b My brother and I _____ for a run every day. (to go)

    c The boy _____ hard for the tests to get full marks. (to study)

    d My sister _____ in a really bad mood if I touch her toys. (to get)

    e The brothers _____ the guitar and keyboard in a rock group. (to play)

    f He usually _____ before breakfast but he woke up too late today. (to swim)

			Total
0		16	
Tough	OK	Got it!	16

Verb tenses

> Verbs in a sentence must always be written in the same tense.
>
> He **went** to the shops and **runs** home. ✗
>   ↑   ↑
> past tense   present tense
>
> He **went** to the shops and **ran** home. ✓ OR He **goes** to the shops and **runs** home. ✓
> ↑   ↑   ↑   ↑
> past tense   past tense   present tense   present tense

1. **Underline the verbs not in the present tense. Write the sentences correctly in the present tense.**

   a I am 10 years old and I enjoyed playing football with my dad.

   _____

   b There are five people in my family and we all ate dinner together.

   _____

   c I liked playing rounders but everyone else likes playing hockey.

   _____

   d People crossed the road when the green man appears.

   _____

2. **Write these sentences in the past tense using the given verbs.**

   a Mel _____ in a show last weekend and she _____ very tired afterwards. (to appear / to be)

   b He _____ his guitar and I _____ to play my keyboard. (to play / to try)

   c The electricians _____ the damaged wiring before they _____ the lights on. (to repair / to switch)

   d We _____ for a walk and I _____ lots of different animals. (to go / to see)

0	Tough	OK	Got it!	8

Total

/8

Sentence types

Sentences have a **different word order** depending on the jobs you want them to do, or the effect you want to create in your writing.

Statement: The boy read his book.

Question: Did the boy read his book?

Order: Read your book!

In each of these sentences, the verbs, nouns and pronouns all move around; the meaning of the sentence changes; and different punctuation is needed.

1. **Turn these questions and statements into orders.**

   a Is it time to leave for the train? _____

   b Could you go now? _____

   c It's time to sit down and eat. _____

   d You can go and play in the garden. _____

2. **Turn these orders into questions.**

   a Stop that noise! _____

   b Don't do that! _____

   c Wait for me! _____

   d Help me! _____

3. **Underline the statements, circle the orders, put a wavy line under the questions and write in all the missing punctuation.** (*10 marks, $\frac{1}{2}$ mark for each*)

   Jonas and Leah were playing in the park Suddenly a man on a motorbike yelled Move

   Leah looked up Why should we We're allowed to play here

   Move now shouted the man It's not safe The frame for that swing is loose

   They looked at the frame and saw it was toppling forwards Run screamed Leah

0	Tough	OK	Got it! 18

Total

/18

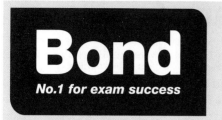

Bond
No.1 for exam success

No Nonsense
English
9–10 years

Parents' notes

What your child will learn from this book

Bond No Nonsense will help your child to understand and become more confident at English. This book features the main English objectives covered by your child's class teacher during the school year. It provides clear, straightforward teaching and learning of the essentials in a rigorous, step-by-step way.

This book begins with some **handwriting practice**. Encourage your child to complete this carefully and to continue writing neatly throughout the book.

The four types of lessons provided are:
Spelling – these cover spelling rules and strategies.
Grammar – these cover word types and sentence construction.
Punctuation – these cover punctuation marks and their rules.
Comprehension – these cover reading different types of text and comprehension questions.

How you can help

Following a few simple guidelines will ensure that your child gets the best from this book:
- Explain that the book will help your child become confident in their English work.
- If your child has difficulty reading the text on the page or understanding a question, do provide help.
- Encourage your child to complete all the exercises in a lesson. You can mark the work using this answer section. Your child can record their own impressions of the work using the 'How did I do?' feature.

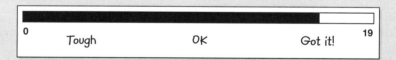

0		
Tough	OK	Got it! 19

- The 'How am I doing?' sections provide a further review of progress.

Don't forget the website . . . !

Visit www.bond11plus.co.uk for lots of advice, information and suggestions on everything to do with Bond, the 11[+] and helping children to achieve their best.

Bond No Nonsense 9–10 years Answers

① Vowel endings p4

1. a banjo b pizza c risotto d ravioli e banana f concerto g cello h pasta i viola j piano k disco l bongo
2. a zebra b kangaroo c cobra
3. a igloos b pianos c echoes d cargoes (sometimes cargos) e mangoes or mangos f cases
4. a tomatoes / avocados b lassos c potatoes

② Plurals p5

1. a leaches b wishes c gases d boxes e suppers f forks
2. a dish b lunch c book d brush e fax f class
3. a berries b cities c crosses d leaves e toys f wives
4. a jelly b half c poppy d life e tray f wolf
5. a calves b seventies c wrappers

③ Prefixes 1 p6

1. a bifocals b television c bilingual d telescope e bicycle
2. a automatic b circumvent c circumnavigate d transform e circumscribe or transcribe f transport g autopsy h transplant i transmit
3. a biplane b autographs c translate d autobiography e television f biceps g circumference

④ Synonyms p7

1. a anger: to make someone very cross
   b irritate: to annoy someone
   c prevent: to stop someone from doing something
   d upset: to cause distress or overturn something
2. a knock / strike / rap / bang / swipe
   b label / sticker / ticket / badge / tag
   c laugh / giggle / chuckle / guffaw / chortle
3. a scene b copying c angry
4. a peckish / hungry / ravenous
   b startled / alarmed / terrified
   c walk / trot / canter / gallop

⑤ Adverbs p8

1. a wearily b politely c noisily d loudly e joyfully f anxiously
2. They all end in 'ly'.
3. a triumphantly b happily c quietly d nastily e calmly f cheerfully
4. a wearily b politely c noisily d excitedly e silently f angrily
5. a excitedly b furiously c gloomily d proudly e sadly

⑥ Root words p9

1. overtake: to catch up and get past
   partake: to get a share in
   mistake: to get something wrong
   bomb: highly explosive materials
   bombastic: pompous speech or writing
   bombardiers: soldiers with heavy weapons
   include: add, join in, be part of
   exclude: keep out or leave out
   seclude: hide from view, keep away
   phone: a telephone
   phoneme: a speech sound
   phoney: not genuine, not real
2. a signal: a sign
   b signature: someone's own handwritten name
   c resigned: given up
   d design: a creation or plan/to plan something
   e insignificant: not important
3. a assistant b government c imprisoned d relation e discovery f forgive

⑦ Changing word order p10

1. a When she opened the door no one was there.
   b With a flurry of wings the birds flew away.
   c Up the tree scrambled a red squirrel.
2. a The rabbit startled the man.
   b Jim raced after the horse.
   c Carole beat Raj in the 100 metre sprint.
3. a, b and c – own answers.

⑧ Editing text p11

1. Possible answers include:
   b I took my umbrella as it was pouring with rain.
   c We went by car although we could have walked home.
   d We couldn't visit Katie as she was ill, so we went to the pictures instead.
2. Possible answers include:
   b The baby's face was covered with chocolate.
   c Kay whispered in Lee's ear, "We should get out, now!"
   d Bev packed lots of clothes for her holiday.

⑨ Speech p12

Possible answers include:
1. a Mum said, "I can't come to the concert because I am working."
   b "Have you forgotten your bus fare, Dinah?" the lady asked.
   c "Do you want to go swimming, Priti?" asked Harry.
   d "Hurry up Belinda, or you will be late," said Mum.
2. a The nurse said good morning to Mr Smith and asked him how he was feeling.
   b Dad reminded me to brush my teeth before I went to bed.
   c Mum whispered at me to be quieter or I would wake the baby.
   d The teacher said to the class that she only wanted to see their best handwriting today and no scribble.

⑩ Auxiliary verbs p13

1. a had b will / should c could d might / are
2. a They are carrying the picnic box. b We are waiting for the bus. c He is cycling around the garden. d I am eating my breakfast.

3. a Claire was doing the washing up. b We had leading roles in the play. c The roadworks were finished. d I was painting a picture.

⑪ First, second and third person p14

1. a They b She c I d you
2. a They went to see Laura today.
   b He/she is running in the race.
   c They chased the cat away.
   d He/she lives in an apartment.
3. a Did you play tennis last week?
   b You will stay at home today.
   c You are nearly as tall as your father.
   d You planted a new lawn.

⑫ Commas and clauses 1 p15

1. a After it raced along the tarmac, the plane took off.
   b Although the skin was bitter, the flesh of the fruit was sweet.
   c As the noise in the tunnel grew louder, the children screamed.
   d So that she could see some lions, Amy went on safari.
2. a Although Brian shouldn't have, he decided to go.
   b Even though she didn't want to, Erin helped her Mum.
   c To get a spanner, Ranjit went to the garage.
   d When I want to be alone, I escape to my bedroom.
3. a ✓ b So he wouldn't be late, Ian ran quickly.
   c If it isn't too cold, we'll play on the swings. d ✓

⑬ Colons, semicolons, hyphens and dashes p16

1. a Here are the directions: leave the M3 at Junction 1 and turn left on to the A308.
   b The presents I still need to buy are: a CD for Ying; a book-token for Gran; and earrings for Mum.
   c Some boys are great footballers; others are not.
   d Shakespeare wrote: 'To be or not to be.'
2. a twenty-one / self-portraits. b three-dimensional c jack-in-the-box d re-sort
3. a melted – the fridge b the dryer – it must have c that house – the one d clouded over – a splatter of

⑭ Dialogue p17

1. a "Don't do that!" said the teacher. "It's dangerous."
   b "Wait!" he yelled. "Come back here!"
   c "It's not fair, I didn't do anything," she wailed.
   d The boy teetered on the edge of the cliff. "Lee!" she shouted. "Don't move!"
2. "You'll never do it," said Josh.
   "You want to bet?" asked Angela.
   "Go on then," he laughed. "See if you can climb that tree. I don't think you will."
   But she did climb the tree and threw the Frisbee back down. "There you are!" she said. "I told you I could do it."
   "Yes, you did tell me but I didn't think you would," he said looking sheepish.
   "Oh well," she said, "at least we got our Frisbee back."

⑮ Story openings p18

1. The story is set on a ship. The ship is about to leave.
2. Own answer but perhaps suggesting that the story starts in a lively way with dialogue and with something about to happen.
3. At nine o'clock on a Wednesday morning at Boston Quay.
4. To England. The journey is three thousand miles.
5. A steam ship: 'the hiss of escaping steam' tells you this.
6. 'like a greyhound at its leash'
7. The hero is a very nervous man. He feels sad. He also feels bitter at having to return home.
8. Because the weather was good for the voyage: 'the sea was calm and the breeze light.'
9. Phrases such as: 'some impending calamity', 'on the verge of great danger', 'the cursed vessel'.
10. Own answer but perhaps suggesting some interest in the unknown and terrible event ahead.

⑯ Recount writing p20

1. a large wildlife area
2. The recount is made up of five paragraphs. The first paragraph gives an overview, or introduction, to the text.
3. Six time connectives: First / Next / After / Lastly / When / Then
4. herbivore / carnivore / (possibly) enclosure / paddock
5. This is a personal account because it is written in the first person and the writer experienced the trip that is being recounted.
6. Yes, because in the last sentence he writes that he thinks this was the best surprise birthday trip he has ever had.
7. Possible answers include:
   a On my birthday I had a surprise trip to a safari park.
   b First we saw giraffes, zebras and flamingos.
   c Then we went to the monkey enclosure.
   d Lastly we saw the lions.
   e It was a great day out.

How am I doing? p22

1. a dominoes b safaris c benches d potatoes e ponies f losses
2. a automatic b circumvent c transform d transplant e circumstance f autopilot g televise h telepathy
3. a cry / sob / wail b whisper / shout / scream c amused / happy / delirious
4. a sweetly b quietly c enthusiastically d calmly e loudly f tentatively
5. a sign b bomb c balance d public
6. a On Monday, we visited Grandma. b Mum cooked some fish for dinner.
7. a "Do you want a cup of tea?" John asked.
   b "Suki is ill and she will not be in school today," the teacher said.

8 a The bus has arrived early. b I was waiting for Oscar.
  c Dad was going to cook dinner.
9 a They went to visit their Grandpa last week.
  b He was riding his bike around the garden.
  c I sat on the chair and it snapped in two!
10 a As it is so hot today, I would like an ice cream.
   b Although it was raining, we decided to go shopping.
   c I saw a kite, which was red and yellow, tangled in a tree.
11 a Inside the package was: a scarf; a packet of biscuits from Gran; and a letter from Mum.
   b Please can we go there – I promise to be good.
   c Wordsworth wrote: "Our souls have sight of that immortal sea".
12 "Where shall we go?" Karisma asked.
   "I don't mind," replied Sophie. "Anywhere you like."
   "I think I'd like to go to the park so we can play on the see-saw," Karisma answered.

(17) Hard and soft c p24

1 soft c: cinema / celery / certain / decimal / lacy / cereal
  hard c: cord / camel / caught / card / culinary / curtain
2 soft c: recite / concert / ceremony / circle / piece
  hard c: concert / Carl / cut / Christmas / cards
3 a cinema b Coventry / City c circulation d bicycle / exercise
  e clothes f carnival / December g couldn't / decide

(18) Common letter strings p25

1 Answers may vary with regional pronunciations.
  oh: bouquet / soul / although   ow: plough / hour / shout
  uh: couple / favour / thorough / aw: yours / mourn / sought
  oo: ghoul / bamboo / cartoon short oo: could / hood / cook
2 a soup / mousse b took / breakthrough c brought / food / mouldy
3 Answers may vary. Examples include:
  look / took / hook / shook   fear / dear / hear / heard

(19) Homophones p26

1 rein / rain / reign   you / yew / ewe
  road / rode / rowed   to / two / too
  by / buy / bye   their / they're / there
  sew / so / sow   cent / scent / sent
2 a beach b great c no d made e main f pane
  g seen h waste i flower j sell k him l hear
3 a deer b through c allowed d vein e piece
4 a key / quay b leek / leak c hair / hare

(20) Possessive pronouns p27

1 I / mine / my   we / ours / our
  you / yours / your   you / yours / your
  he, she, it / his, hers, its / his, her, its   they / theirs / their
2 a their / their b your / his / yours c its / ours d our / my
3 a its b your c his d her e its f your

(21) Suffixes p28

1 a explosion b transfusion c promotion d electrician
  e direction f politician g connection h completion
  i discussion j magician
2 a collision b optician c physician d provisions
  e reduction f possessions g permission / television
  h demonstration / devotion
3 a electrician b ✓ c decision d permission

(22) Onomatopoeia p29

1 twitter / miaow / growl / croak / tweet / yelp / hoot / crunch / woof / splash
2 a buzz: the sound a bee makes when it flies
  b slurp: the sound of someone eating soup messily
  c thud: the noise when something heavy falls on the floor
3 a hiss / slithered b whizzed / fizzled c sizzled / splattered d popped / fizzed
4 Possible answers include:
  a buzzed b squelched c squealed d quacked

(23) Grammatical agreement p30

1 a swings / swing b coughs / cough c sing / sings
2 a uses b live c cross d grow e empties f Do
  g chews
3 a walks b go c studies d gets e play f swims

(24) Verb tenses p31

1 a enjoyed: I am 10 years old and I enjoy playing football with my dad.
  b ate: There are five people in my family and we all eat dinner together.
  c liked: I like playing rounders but everyone else likes playing hockey.
  d crossed: People cross the road when the green man appears.
2 a appeared / was b played / tried c repaired / switched d went / saw

(25) Sentence types p32

1 Possible answers include:
  a It is time to leave for the train! b Go now!
  c Sit down and eat! d Go and play in the garden!
2 a Can you stop that noise? b Could you not do that?
  c Could you wait for me? d Could you help me?
3 Jonas and Leah were playing in the park. Suddenly a man on a motorbike yelled, "Move!" Leah looked up. "Why should we? We're allowed to play here."
  "Move now!" shouted the man. "It's not safe. The frame for that swing is loose."
  They looked at the frame and saw it was toppling forwards. "Run!" screamed Leah.

(26) Adapting texts 1 p33

1 Possible answer:
  Julie went for a ride on her bike. She rode across the yard. She rode over the bridge. She rode down the path. She rode through the puddles. She rode under the washing and arrived home in time for tea.

2 Possible answer:
  Billy was boiling as he ambled along the narrow street.
  As he walked, he started to dream of cold things. "I really wish I had an ice cream – that would cool me down!" he said out loud to a passing seagull.
  Billy continued down the road and bumped into his best friend, Ali, and her mum. "Hello Billy. How are you?" asked Ali's mum.
  "I am very hot and wish I had an ice cream right now!" replied Billy.
  "You shouldn't have an ice cream, Billy, it would spoil your dinner!" answered Ali's mum.

(27) Ambiguities p34

1 a The toilet is for disabled people. b The toilet is not working.
2 Possible answers include:
  a A man who had a knife was shot by the police.
  b A stolen painting was found beside a tree.
3 Possible answers include:
  a In my pyjamas, I read a story about an elephant.
  b I would like to eat an ice lolly because I am so hot.
  c I know a man who has a dog that has fleas.

(28) Sentence structure p35

1 a When Emily looked down, she could see lots of tiny cars, buses and houses.
  b Even though Tom kept telling it not to, the cat sat on the bed.
2 a I put on my swimming trunks, left the cubicle and dived into the cool water.
  b Turn left at the roundabout, turn right at the traffic lights and then stop at number 21.
3 Chloe really enjoyed walking her little brown Jack Russell in the local park. When they walked through the rusty park gates, Jekyl, her dog, always barked at the squirrels.

(29) Indicating intonation p36

1 a I saw John at the circus – and he wasn't by himself!
  b I promise that I won't tell anyone – until tonight!
  c Thanks – I'd love to go with you!
2 a You will be walking the dog later! / You will be walking the dog later?
  b We are going back to the classroom! / We are going back to the classroom?
  c You will take the basketball outside! / You will take the basketball outside?
  d He is walking home from school! / He is walking home from school?

(30) Commas and clauses 2 p37

1 a which were in a blue vase The flowers smelled beautiful.
  b whose name is Sally My aunt lives in Australia.
  c as I discovered yesterday There is a funfair in town.
2 a High on the mountains in Tibet, in the thick bamboo forests, live giant pandas.
  b Camels, with their soft wide feet, are able to walk on the sand quite easily.
  c Alan, using his new building set, made a castle with a tall tower.
3 a One night, although it was late, they stopped to look at the stars.
  b Mum rocked the baby then, when he had dropped off to sleep, put him in his cot.

(31) Narrative poetry p38

1 He was a very experienced seaman.
2 He could not see the moon.
3 the daughter
4 Probably a light on the shore.
5 stiff and stark
6 'like a frighted steed' / 'Like the horns of an angry bull'
7 They looked 'soft as fine combed wool'.
8 The skipper for not listening to the old sailor.

(32) Taking notes p40

1 a on a school trip b she was sick on the train
2 No the notes are not in a logical or chronological order. Although most notes include times, they have been written down in the wrong order. For example, the second note should come before the first point as it happened 30 minutes earlier.
3 Yr (Year); mins (minutes); NB (abbreviation for a Latin phrase, *nota bene*, which is used to draw attention to a specific point); re (means with reference to, concerning); SM (Science Museum); sci (science); tech (technology); trans (transport)
4 Notes could have been written in chronological order; bullet points could have been used to make individual notes clearer; each new point could have been started on a new line.
5 Technical language could have been introduced in a discussion of the collections that were seen in the museum.
6 The journey to the museum could have been covered in one or two points, so that more notes could have been used to record what was seen and experienced in the Science Museum. There is a lot of key information and detail missing from this section of the visit, which is likely to be needed in follow-up work.

How am I doing? p42

1 a ceremony b catch / cold c scored / century
2 oh: bouquet / soul ow: drought / sour uh: borough / couple
  aw: mourn / bought oo: food / through short oo: good / cook
3 a cell b flour c wait d him e vein / vane f sum
  g tail h deer
4 a mine b their / their c your
5 a succession b musician c explosion d distribution e action f electrician
6 whizz / bang pop / crackle / slither
7 a watches b will visit
8 a I like this one but it is your choice.
  b We are trying to make a model of an aeroplane but I can't follow the instructions.
9 a Are you going to stop that? b Shall we walk home now? c Can you wait there?
10 a Fish can make the best sandwiches. b Fish is the best sandwich filling.
11 I cut the cheese, put it on the roll, spread the pickle and ate my sandwich.
12 a I saw Tilly at the cinema – and she was with Paul!
   b I promise that I won't tell anyone – yet!
13 a Ranjif, who had always been good at sport, came first in the cross country race.
   b I saw a kite, which was red and yellow, tangled in a tree.

(33) Antonyms p44

1 old / young   near / far   light / dark
  hot / cold   happy / sad   small / big
  clean / dirty   timid / bold   fade / brighten
  find / lose   low / high   oral / written
2 a safe b sour c best d right

3 a ✓ b ✗ c ✓ d ✓ e ✗ f ✗
   g ✗ h ✓ i ✓ j ✗
4 a wrong / left b heavy / dark c rich / good d dark / stupid
5 a wide / narrow b long / short
   c heavy / light d beginning / end

34 Unstressed vowels p45

1 a list / <u>en</u> / ing b his / t<u>or</u> / y c dif / f<u>er</u> /ence
   d li / br<u>a</u> / ry e Feb / r<u>u</u> /ary f strength / <u>en</u>
2 a offering b fastener c factory d desperate e brightening
   f general g voluntary h boundary i conference
3 a different b dictionary c forgotten
4 a hospital b separate c carpet

35 Letter strings – ie and ei p46

1 mischief / deceive / ceiling / shield / patient / conceit / friendship / achieve
2 a either b pie c receipt d died e eighth f lie
3 a briefcase b leisure c weird d received e height f field g veil

36 Prefixes 2 p47

1 a incomplete b inactive c impossible d incorrect e immature
   f inexpensive g inhuman h impatient
2 a illiterate b irrational c illegal d illegible e irresponsible f irregular
3 a indecisive b impolite c inconvenient d impractical

37 Borrowed words p48

1 a cul-de-sac: dead-end street, France
   b spaghetti: long solid strings of flour paste, Italy
   c matinee: afternoon performance of a play or a film, France
   d pasta: shapes of dough made from flour and water, Italy
   e pizza: baked dough crust with tasty topping, Italy
   f tableau: still scene formed by living people, France
2 a kangaroo / Australia b macaroni / Italy c koalas / Australia
   d bungalow / India e biryani / India f pyjamas / India
   g chalet / France h cargo / Spain i chow mein / China j adieu / France

38 Shortened words p49

1 bus / omnibus phone / telephone bike / bicycle
   photo / photograph rhino / rhinoceros
2 MD: managing director PC: personal computer MP: member of parliament
   PE: physical education HGV: heavy goods vehicle
3 a United Kingdom b aeroplane c doctor
   d United States of America e frequently asked questions f very important person
4 a fridge b bbq c stereo

39 Conjunctions p50

1 a I was very embarrassed because I was the last person to arrive.
   b I could stay at home or I could go out.
   c I waited for my mum outside while she went to the post office.
   d Six of us were going bowling but only five of us turned up.
   e I was eating my dinner when the telephone rang.
2 Possible answers include:
   b It was cold when Katy went out but she found a beautiful ring.
   c Because it was cold Katy went out and found a beautiful ring.
   d While it was cold, Katy went out and she found a beautiful ring.
   e Although it was cold when Katy went out she found a beautiful ring.

40 Double negatives p51

1 a Nobody's ever been into that house. b Tom's never done anything to upset him.
   c I can't do any of these sums. d You're not doing anything wrong are you?
   e Mary is ill; she doesn't want any dinner.
2 a ✓ b no / nothing – anything c don't / none – any d aren't / no – any e ✓
3 a I didn't see anything! / I saw nothing.
   b He never smiles at anyone. / He smiles at no one.
   c I didn't get any answer. / I got no answer.
   d Steve didn't get any. / Steve got none.
   e This film isn't any good. / This film is no good.

41 Adapting texts 2 p52

1 a donnies b ain't / arf / 'ere c barmy
   d Gerr / larkin e babbee / mooch f bloke
2 Possible answer:
   The snow was everywhere you looked. It had completely covered the M25 – the motorway that went around the outside of London. This motorway was normally full of traffic and noise but as it was covered in snow, there was no traffic and everywhere was silent. The sun would soon melt the snow, but for now it was a wonderful sight.

42 Prepositions p53

1 about / past / against / onto / among / at / behind / beside / between / under / now / by / down / during / upon / for / from / into / near / of / off / out / underneath / over / since / through / towards / throughout
2 a Noun: picture; Pronoun: I / I; Preposition: Before
   b Noun: Jack / beanstalk; Preposition: up / to
   c Noun: path / river; Pronoun: We; Preposition: along / to
   d Noun: dog / rabbit / common; Preposition: across
   e Noun: earth / sun / day; Preposition: around
3 a on b At / below c with / in / to d above / beyond

43 Clauses p54

1 a Subordinate clause: While Mum was driving.
   b Subordinate clause: because I want to learn a new language
   c Subordinate clause: while they are getting better every day
   d Subordinate clause: After I got home from school
2 Possible answers include:
   a Even though we didn't have much, we shared our food.
   b When I have time, I like reading stories.
   c After they had finished shopping, they had a cup of coffee.
   d Until you hand in your homework, I can't give you a mark.

44 Punctuating sentences p55

1 a Bev, if you take too long to get dressed, you'll be late for school.
   b When the whistle blew, everyone sprinted down the track.
   c If it doesn't rain this afternoon, we'll go to the park.
   d I turned away, after hugging Mum tightly, and got on the bus.
   e If I can, I'll come and visit you.
   f Trisha, who was 10, helped Michael up the stairs.
2 a "Tomorrow, bright and early, we leave for Florida."
   b "How long will you be?" asked Mum. "It's time we were off."
   c "She's gone now," thought Sarah, "but for how long?"
   d Needless to say, with all the excitement, she forgot her promise.

45 Apostrophes p56

1 a the boy's ruler b three boys' rulers
   c the dog's bone d two dogs' bones
   e the squirrel's tail f five squirrels' tails
   g the bus' wheels h four buses' wheels
2 a the person's food b the people's food
   c the man's team d the men's team
   e the woman's clothes f the women's clothes
   g the child's toys h the children's toys
3 b She borrowed Tina's cardigan. c We stroked Raul and Natalia's dog.
   d Jerry opened the budgie's cage. e We went to Toby's house.

46 Brackets and dashes p57

1 a I looked inside the cage for Polly – she wasn't there!
   b Come at 2 – I'll be ready.
   c Stay a little longer – you know you want to.
   d The door creaked open slowly – what lay inside?
2 a Inside the parcel was a scarf – a soft red one – from Auntie Jo.
   b She unwrapped the chocolate – the only one left – and put it in her mouth.
   c No one – not even Ben – was strong enough to lift the bench.
   d There were two people – Akash and Stuart – in front of me in the dinner queue.
3 a Jacqueline Wilson (author of several books) is coming to our town tomorrow.
   b The A380 (an aeroplane) is as long as a football pitch.
   c His new car (a VW Golf) was a lovely ocean green colour.
   d I didn't see him do it (I was looking the other way at the time) but I know it was him.

47 Stories from different places p58

1 A fairy or folk story because of its opening: 'Once, a long time ago…'
2 The story uses unusual words (dialect words).
3 a girl b a good house c mistreated / treated badly
4 The lassie
5 Yule is Christmas
6 a stayed b knew c church
7 Cinderella
8 Answers might include the following:
   Name: Rashin-Coatie / Cinderella; Number of ugly sisters: 1 / 2; Helper in the story: calf / fairy godmother; Place where everyone goes when the girl is left behind: kirk / ball; Reason for leaving: to cook dinner / midnight; Method of getting home afterwards: walks / coach; etc.

48 Objective or subjective? p60

1 Text A appears to be objective; text B appears to be subjective.
2 The fact that many local jobs will be created by the development of the road has been omitted from text B. This has been left out so no positive points are included in the account in B.
3 The real truth is …
4 Powerful verbs: force / lose / destroyed / coated / destroyed / deluded / increases / defiling / bulldozed / destroyed
   Rhetorical questions: but at what cost? / And what of the ancient roadways? / Are you expected to just sit back and watch them be destroyed? / Surely the council must be deluded if it really thinks this new road will keep traffic away from the city? / Do we really want all that noise and pollution defiling our beautiful countryside?
5 Whole / Countless
6 Hundreds of homeowners / developers' demolition / fields of fertile farmland / coated in concrete
7 Capital letters have been used to add further emphasis and to call out to the reader in order to provoke a personal and emotional response.
8 Text A is likely to have been written by a reporter rather than a member of the council as it appears to be putting forward facts, not trying to persuade the reader to one point of view.
   Text B is likely to have been written by a village member, as it presents a very negative and emotional view of the situation.
9 Neither text presents a full picture of the potential road development, as both texts exclude information that is included in the other text. Text A mentions that jobs will be created; text B mentions the destruction of farmland and roads.

How am I doing? p62

1 a good b difficult c expensive d near
2 a voluntary b frightening c mystery d difference e listening f category
   g generous h diary
3 a science b glacier c ancient d weird e eighth f tie
   g either h handkerchief
4 a implant b incorrect c indefinite d invisible e irrational
   f illegible g illicit h imbalance
5 a anorak b canoe c giraffe d kindergarten
6 a B&B b hippo c plane d DIY e PTO f photo
7 Possible answers include:
   a but b or c so
8 a No one has ever seen it! b We aren't going any more. c I have never done that.
9 a under / near b down / beside / across / to
   c along / through / towards
10 a when she came off the phone b Although it was nearly dinner time
   c After we had seen Granny
11 a The men's coats. b The girls' glasses. c The dogs' tails.
12 a Charles Dickens (1812–1870) wrote many fine novels.
   b He looked up slowly – what was it?
   c He bought: a bunch of bananas; a punnet of raspberries; and two plums for dessert.

Adapting texts 1

When authors write books, they must match their writing to their **audience**.

Books for **young children** have short, **simple sentences**, **repeated phrases** and short, **easy words**.

Books for **older children** have detailed sentences, harder words to read and many more pages.

1. **Rewrite this to make it suitable for a younger child to read.** *(5 marks)*

Julie went for an adventure on her wonderful new bike. She rode across the middle of the yard, over the crumbling, ancient bridge, along the winding path, through the numerous puddles, underneath the fresh washing and arrived home in time for tea.

Julie went for a ride on her bike. She

_____

_____

_____

and arrived home in time for tea.

2. **Rewrite this story to make it interesting for an older child.** *(5 marks)*

Billy walked down the street. He was hot.

"I wish I had an ice cream," he said to the seagull.

Then Billy saw his best friend Ali with her mum.

"I wish I had an ice cream," he said to Ali's mum.

"It will spoil your dinner!" said Ali's mum.

_____

_____

_____

_____

_____

_____

0			10
Tough	OK	Got it!	

Total

/10

Ambiguities

> **Ambiguities** are sentences or phrases that can have more than one meaning.
> Labels and newspaper headlines give information in as few words as possible. This
> can lead to phrases that are confusing and ambiguous:
>
> | BABY CHANGING |
> | ROOM |
>
> Is this the room where a baby's nappy is changed or something more sinister – a room
> where one baby can be changed for another?

1. **Write two meanings for this sign.** (DISABLED TOILET)

   a _____

   b _____

2. **Write these headlines as full sentences so we know what they really mean.**

   a Police shot man with a knife!

   _____

   _____

   b Stolen painting found by tree!

   _____

   _____

3. **Rewrite these sentences to make their meaning clear.**

   a I read a story about an elephant in my pyjamas.

   _____

   b I feel like an ice lolly because I'm so hot.

   _____

   c I know a man with a dog who has fleas.

   _____

0			7
Tough	OK	Got it!	

Total

7

34

Sentence structure

Sentences can be structured in **different ways** but still keep the **same meaning**.

I play netball every Tuesday.
Every Tuesday, I play netball.

Two or more sentences can be **combined** to make a more **complex** sentence.

At full moon the highest tides occur. This means bigger waves.
At full moon the highest tides occur, resulting in bigger waves.

Words can be **deleted** or **replaced** to improve clarity or shorten sentences.

Not always, just every now and then, she went to the nearby park.
Every now and then, she went to the local park.

1. **Reorder each sentence without changing the meaning.**

   a Emily could see lots of tiny cars, buses and houses when she looked down.

   _____

   b The cat sat on the bed even though Tom kept telling it not to.

   _____

2. **Rewrite these sentences as one sentence. Delete or add extra words if you need to.**

   a I put on my swimming trunks. I left the cubicle. I dived into the cool water.

   _____

   b Turn left at the roundabout. Turn right at the traffic lights. Stop at number 21.

   _____

3. **Cross out unnecessary words but keep the meaning the same. Write the new sentences.** (4 marks, $\frac{1}{2}$ mark for each)

   Chloe really enjoyed walking her little brown Jack Russell in the local park. When they walked through the rusty park gates, Jekyl, her dog, always barked at the squirrels.

   _____

   _____

0			8	Total
Tough	OK	Got it!		

Indicating intonation

Gestures, **facial expressions** and **intonation** help with expression when someone speaks. In writing, **punctuation** can help to show how something is said.

Question marks and exclamation marks tell us to say the same sentence in different ways:
> You are going to Gran's after school.　　**statement**
> You are going to Gran's after school**?**　**question**
> You are going to Gran's after school**!**　**order**

Exclamation marks can also be used to show **surprise**.

Dashes can be used to show long **pauses** in speech:
"We are going to Gran's – after school," Mum told Stephen.

1.　**Rewrite these statements, expressing surprise and using pauses.**

   a I saw John at the circus and he wasn't by himself.

   _____

   b I promise that I won't tell anyone until tonight.

   _____

   c Thanks I'd love to go with you.

   _____

2.　**Using punctuation, change each statement first into an order, then a question.**

   a You will be walking the dog later.

   _____　　_____

   b We are going back to the classroom.

   _____　　_____

   c You will take the basketball outside.

   _____　　_____

   d He is walking home from school.

   _____　　_____

0			7	Total
Tough	OK	Got it!		/7

Commas and clauses 2

A **subordinate clause** can be **embedded** in the middle of a main clause. A comma is needed either side of the subordinate clause:

subordinate clause

↑

The tree, <u>which was old and rotten</u>, had fallen over.

Main clause: The tree had fallen over.

QUICK TIP!
The main clause makes sense by itself.

1. **Underline the subordinate clause in each sentence and write the main clause.**

   a The flowers, which were in a blue vase, smelled beautiful.

   _____

   b My aunt, whose name is Sally, lives in Australia.

   _____

   c There is, as I discovered yesterday, a funfair in town.

   _____

2. **Add the missing commas to these sentences.**

   a High on the mountains in Tibet in the thick bamboo forests live giant pandas.

   b Camels with their soft wide feet are able to walk on the sand quite easily.

   c Alan using his new building set made a castle with a tall tower.

3. **Embed the subordinate clauses in the main clauses.**

   a Main clause: One night they stopped to look at the stars.
   Subordinate clause: although it was late
   _One night, although_____

   b Main clause: Mum rocked the baby then put him in his cot.
   Subordinate clause: when he had dropped off to sleep

   _____

0			8
Tough	OK	Got it!	

Total

8

37

Narrative poetry

A **narrative poem** is a poem that tells a story.

Read these extracts from a narrative poem twice. Then answer the questions.

The sailing ship *Hesperus* sets off on a winter voyage. The captain takes his young daughter with him. They haven't gone very far when:

Then up spoke an old sailor,
Had sailed to the Spanish Main,
"I pray you, put into yonder port,
For I fear a hurricane.
Last night, the moon had a golden ring,
And to-night no moon we see!"
The skipper, he blew a whiff from his pipe,
And a scornful laugh laughed he.

Sure enough, a storm strikes the ship:

Down came the storm, and struck hard
The vessel in its strength;
She shuddered and paused, like a frighted steed,
Then leaped her cable's length.
"O Father! I see a gleaming light,
Oh say, what may it be?"
But the father answered never a word,
A frozen corpse was he.
Lashed to the helm, all stiff and stark,
With his face turned to the skies,
The lantern gleamed through the gleaming snow
On his fixed and glassy eyes.

The Hesperus drifts, 'like a sheeted ghost', onto a reef:

She struck where the white and fleecy waves
Looked soft as fine combed wool,
But the cruel rocks, they gored her side
Like the horns of an angry bull.
Her rattling shrouds, all covered in ice,
With the masts went by the board;
Like a vessel of glass, she shattered and sank,
Ho! ho! the breakers roared!

1. **Circle the correct answer.**

   Why should the skipper have believed the sailor? Because:

   he was Spanish   he was on deck   he was older   he was a very experienced seaman

2. **How did the sailor know a hurricane was coming?**

   _____

3. **Who says 'O Father! I see a gleaming light?' Circle the correct answer.**

   The skipper   the sailor   a ghost   the daughter

4. **What do you think the gleaming light was?**

   _____

5. **Write down the alliterative phrase that describes the skipper's frozen corpse?**

   _____

6. **Write down the two similes that compare the ship and the rocks to animals.**

   _____

   _____

7. **The waves on the shore don't look dangerous. How do we know?**

   _____

   _____

8. **Who was really responsible for not preventing the disaster? Can you say why?**

   _____

   _____

			Total
0 Tough	OK	Got it! 8	8

39

Taking notes

When we listen to information, it is useful to take **notes** to make sure that we can **remember** what we have heard.

Here are some simple guidelines, which can help you improve your note-taking skills:

1 Only write down the **main points** or key pieces of information.
2 Write down any **technical language** or terms used.
3 Record points in **chronological order**.
4 Write **short** notes, using **abbreviations**.
5 Use a clear and **structured layout**.
6 Start a **new line** for each new point.
7 Use **symbols** or **bullet points** to separate key details.

As we all have different styles of note-taking, you should make sure your notes are in a **clear format** before giving them to others to read.

Read these notes and then answer the questions.

16/07/05

Science Museum trip, London / Yr 5

coach late, arrived 8.45am

8.15am children assembled

missed 9.00am train – 30 mins wait

arrived Paddington, 11.30am

Ellie ill on train – NB talk to Ellie's mum re travel sickness remedies for next trip! underground tube trains – delays! lunch Hyde Park, 12.30pm

Johnny forgot packed lunch again – NB talk to Johnny's mum re trip rules!

arrived SM, 1.30pm

split Yr 5 into 3 groups, 1 guide each

saw collections for environmental sci. / space tech. / road trans. / water trans.

Re-grouped, 3pm / train – 4pm

Ellie ill again! NB REMEMBER to talk to Ellie's mum

Coach on time – back 6.30pm

1. **Circle the correct answers.**

   a When were these notes taken?

   on a school trip   during a football match   at a concert

   b What was wrong with Ellie?

   she lost her lunchbox   she was sick on the train   she joined the wrong group

2. **Do the notes follow a logical and chronological order? Explain your answer.**

   _____

   _____

3. **What abbreviations does the writer use and what do they stand for?**

   (4 marks, $\frac{1}{2}$ mark for each)

   _____

   _____

4. **How could the layout have been more clearly structured?**

   _____

   _____

5. **Where could the writer have introduced technical language?**

   _____

   _____

6. **How could the content of the notes have been improved?**

   _____

   _____

   _____

			Total
0 Tough	OK	Got it! 10	/10

How am I doing?

1. **Underline the misspelt words and write the correct spellings.**

   a We watched the awards seremony last night. _____

   b Jason didn't want to katch his sister's kold. _____

   c The batsman skored a sentury in the match. _____

2. **Group these words together by their pronunciation.** (*6 marks, ½ mark for each*)

   bouquet food drought mourn borough soul good bought couple through sour cook

oh	ow	uh	aw	oo	short oo

3. **Write a homophone for each of these words.**

   a sell _____   b flower _____   c weight _____   d hymn _____

   e vain _____   f some _____   g tale _____   h dear _____

4. **Complete these sentences with possessive pronouns.**

   a Kira took her book home and said happily, "This book is _____!"

   b They walked to _____ house where _____ Dad was waiting for them.

   c "Could you please hand in _____ homework, Keisha?" asked Mrs White.

5. **Write these words with the correct suffix.**

   tion   sion   ssion   cian

   a success_____   b music_____   c explode_____

   d distribute_____   e act_____   f electric _____

6. **Circle the onomatopoeic words in the list below.**

   whizz table bang pop path crackle car girl slither house

7. **Choose the correct verb tense and ending to agree with the rest of the sentence.**

   a He always _____ rugby every Sunday. (to watch)

   b She _____ her aunt tomorrow. (to visit)

8. Rewrite these sentences so that all verbs are in the present tense.

a I like this one but it was your choice.

_____

b We are trying to make a model of an aeroplane but I couldn't follow the instructions.

_____

9. Turn these orders into questions.

a You are going to stop that! _____

b Walk home now! _____

c Wait there! _____

10. Write two possible interpretations of this sentence:

Fish makes best sandwiches!

a _____

b _____

11. Rewrite these short sentences as one longer one – add extra words if you need them.

I cut the cheese. I put the cheese on the roll. I spread the pickle. I ate my sandwich.

_____

_____

12. Rewrite these statements, expressing surprise and adding pauses.

a I saw Tilly at the cinema and she was with Paul.

_____

b I promise that I won't tell anyone yet.

_____

13. Separate the main and subordinate clauses with commas.

a Ranjif who had always been good at sport came first in the cross country race.

b I saw a kite which was red and yellow tangled in a tree.

Total

41

Antonyms

> The word **antonym** means **opposite**: an antonym of **good** is **bad**.
> Some words have more than one antonym: **soft** and **easy** are both antonyms of **hard**.
> Some words have no antonyms: **green**.

1. **Join the pairs of antonyms.** *(11 marks)*

old	cold	happy	bold	fade	written
near	dark	small	dirty	find	high
light	young	clean	sad	low	lose
hot	far	timid	big	oral	brighten

2. **Rewrite these sentences, changing each word for its antonym.**

   a It was a **dangerous** place to climb. _____

   b The fruit crumble was very **sweet**. _____

   c It was the **worst** day of his life. _____

   d She knew it was the **wrong** thing to do. _____

3. **Tick ✓ the words which have antonyms and cross ✗ the words which do not.**

   a awake ___   b blood ___   c quiet ___   d careless ___   e wall ___

   f line ___   g bottle ___   h rough ___   i fast ___   j glass ___

4. **Write two antonyms for each word.**

   a right _____ _____   b light _____ _____

   c poor _____ _____   d bright _____ _____

5. **Complete each sentence with a pair of antonyms from the list below.**

   long wide beginning heavy light narrow short end

   a The car was _____ and the gap was too _____ to drive through.

   b She wanted to keep her hair _____ but her Mum cut it _____.

   c The case looked _____ but it was surprisingly _____.

   d A list of contents is at the _____ of a book and the index is at the _____.

0			33
Tough	OK	Got it!	

Total

33 / 33

44

Unstressed vowels

The vowels in some words with two or more syllables can be difficult to hear (unstressed vowels). It can make the words difficult to spell.

interesting sounds like **intresting**

Pronouncing each syllable clearly makes them easier to spell:

in / **ter** / est / ing

1. **Split these words into syllables, then underline the unstressed vowels.**

    a listening _____

    b history _____

    c difference _____

    d library _____

    e February _____

    f strengthen _____

2. **Spell these words correctly, putting in the missing unstressed vowels.**

    a offring _____

    b fastner _____

    c factry _____

    d desprate _____

    e brightning _____

    f genral _____

    g voluntry _____

    h boundry _____

    i confrence _____

3. **Underline the words spelt incorrectly in these sentences and write them correctly.**

    a Jon came to a totally diffrent answer from me. _____

    b A dictionry is useful for looking up information about words. _____

    c Samir had forgottn his homework. _____

Mnemonics can make it easier to remember how to spell words.

An **en**velope is a piece of station**ery**.

A **car** that is not moving is station**ary**.

---

4. **Complete the mnemonics using these words.**

    separate   carpet   hospital

    a **Al** is in _____ .

    b There is **a rat** in _____ .

    c Whose **pet** is on the _____ ?

Letter strings – ie and ei

In words which have **i** and **e** together, the rule is:
  i before **e** except after **c**
This is true for most words when the letters make an **ee** sound:
  si**e**ge   dec**ei**t
There are **exceptions** to the rule and these must be learned.
If the letters make a long **a** sound, the spelling is usually **ei**:
  w**ei**ght   n**ei**ghbour

> **QUICK TIP!**
> Words can **only**
> **end** in ie (**tie**)
> and can **only start**
> with ei (**eight**).

1. **Circle the eight misspelt words and then write them correctly.**

   mischeif   decieve   diesel   cieling   fierce   sheild   pateint

   conciet   review   quiet   freindship   belief   siesta   acheive

   _____   _____   _____   _____

   _____   _____   _____   _____

2. **Complete these words using ei or ie.**

   a ____ther   **b** p____   **c** rec_____ pt   **d** d___d   **e** ____ghth   **f** l____

3. **Complete each sentence with a word that uses ei or ie and has a similar meaning to the words in brackets.**

   a She placed the papers in her br_____case. (bag)

   b I decided I would telephone her at my l_____. (free time)

   c The bell made a w_____ booming sound when we pushed it. (strange)

   d He r_____ a large parcel through the post on his birthday. (was given)

   e The nurse measured my h_____ during my examination. (how tall)

   f The farmer ploughed his f_____ so he could sow the seeds. (meadow)

   g The bride wore a v_____ over her face as she walked down the aisle. (mask)

0			21	Total
Tough	OK	Got it!		

Prefixes 2

> **Prefixes** are put at the beginning of words to change their meaning.
>
> The prefixes **in**, **im**, **ir** and **il** give a word the **opposite** meaning.
>
> Add **in** for most words:
> **in**accurate = **not** accurate **in**consistent = **not** consistent
>
> Apart from words beginning with:
> * **b**, **p** or **m**   add **im**   **im**proper = **not** proper
> * **l**   add **il**   **il**logical = **not** logical
> * **r**   add **ir**   **ir**relevant = **not** relevant

1. **Add the prefix in or im to these words.**

   a _____complete   **b** _____active   **c** _____possible   **d** _____correct

   e _____mature   **f** _____expensive **g** _____human   **h** _____patient

2. **Write the correct spellings for these misspelt words.**

   a irliterate _____   **b** inrational _____

   c imlegal _____   **d** imlegible _____

   e ilresponsible _____   **f** ilregular _____

3. **Write these words using the correct prefix and then use the new words to complete the sentences.**

   polite   decisive   practical   convenient

   _____   _____

   _____   _____

   a If you cannot make up your mind you are being _____ .

   b It is _____ not to say thank you after someone has done something for you.

   c I'm sorry but I cannot see you at that time as it is _____ for me.

   d It is _____ to wear sandals in the rain as you will get wet feet!

0			18
Tough	OK	Got it!	

Total

/18

Borrowed words

Lots of words in English have come from other countries:

China (**kung-fu**)   France (**crayon**)   Germany (**glockenspiel**)
India (**dinghy**)   Italy (**umbrella**)   Japan (**origami**)

1. **Match these words with their meanings and the country they came from.**

Word	**Meaning**	**Country of origin**
a cul-de-sac	baked dough crust with tasty topping	Italy
b spaghetti	dead-end street	France
c matinee	shapes of dough made from flour and water	France
d pasta	still scene formed by living people	Italy
e pizza	long solid strings of flour paste	France
f tableau	afternoon performance of a play or a film	Italy

2. **Complete the sentences using these words. Write which country (Australia, France, India, China, Spain) the word comes from at the end of the sentence.**

koalas   adieu   macaroni   kangaroo   pyjamas
biryani   chalet   chow mein   cargo   bungalow

a A _____ often balances on its back legs and sturdy tail. _Australia_

b _____ is often served in a cheese sauce. _____

c _____ are often called bears but they are marsupials. _____

d A _____ is a single-storey house. _____

e _____ is a dish of highly flavoured rice and meat. _____

f _____ are clothes you wear in bed. _____

g A _____ is a house with a gently sloping, overhanging roof. _____

h Some ships carry _____ to transport it from place to place. _____

i _____ is a dish of meat, vegetables and fried noodles. _____

j Farewell, cheerio and _____ all mean 'goodbye'. _____

0			16
Tough	OK	Got it!	

Total
/16

Shortened words

English is always changing. **New** words are formed; words are **abbreviated** to shorter versions or to their initials (**acronyms**).

Abbreviation: examination = exam   **Acronym**: compact disc = CD

1. **Match these abbreviated words with their original word forms.**

   bus   photograph

   phone   rhinoceros

   bike   telephone

   photo   omnibus

   rhino   bicycle

2. **Match these acronyms with the word cluster they represent.**

   MD   heavy goods vehicle

   PC   managing director

   MP   physical education

   PE   personal computer or police constable

   HGV   member of parliament

3. **Write the longer forms of these abbreviations and acronyms.**

   a UK _____   **b** plane _____

   c Dr _____   **d** USA _____

   e FAQ _____   **f** VIP _____

4. **Complete these sentences with the abbreviated forms of the words below.**

   stereo system barbeque refrigerator

   a We put food that needs to be kept cold in the _____.

   b I love cooking and eating outside, so I have just bought a new _____.

   c They enjoyed listening to CDs on their _____.

0		11
Tough	OK	Got it!

Total

/11

Conjunctions

> **Conjunctions** are words that join sentences.
>
> It was incredibly cold outside. I was beginning to shiver.
> It was incredibly cold outside **so** I was beginning to shiver.
> It was incredibly cold outside **and** I was beginning to shiver.
> I was beginning to shiver **because** it was incredibly cold outside.

1. **Use these conjunctions to join the sentences.**

   but   or   when   because   while

   a I was very embarrassed. I was the last person to arrive.

   _____

   b I could stay at home. I could go out.

   _____

   c I waited for my mum outside. She went into the post office.

   _____

   d Six of us were going to go bowling. Only five of us turned up.

   _____

   e I was eating my dinner. The telephone rang.

   _____

2. **Join these three short sentences in as many ways as possible using different conjunctions.**

   | It was cold. | | Katy went for a walk. | | She found a beautiful ring. |

   The meaning must stay the same but you can replace words and leave some out.

   a _It was cold but Katy went for a walk and found a beautiful ring._

   b _____

   c _____

   d _____

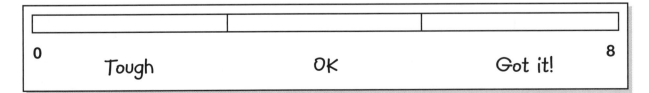

| 0 | | | 8 |
| Tough | OK | Got it! | |

Total

8

Double negatives

> If you use **two negative words** they cancel each other out.
>   "You're **not** doing **nothing**."
>
> To say the same thing but make the sentence correct it should be:
>   "You're not doing anything."   OR   "You're doing nothing."

1. **Rewrite the sentences, replacing the highlighted negative word so that the meaning is clear.**

  a Nobody's **never** been into that house. _____

  b Tom's never done **nothing** to upset him. _____

  c I can't do **none** of these sums. _____

  d You're not doing **nothing** wrong are you? _____

  e Mary is ill; she doesn't want **no** dinner. _____

2. **If a sentence is correct give it a tick ✓. If it is wrong, circle both the negatives and write the correct word to replace one of them.**

  a I can't see any crabs in the pool. _____

  b There's no time for nothing these days. _____

  c I don't want none of those squirrels on my roof. _____

  d We aren't going to no football matches this year. _____

3. **Rewrite these sentences correctly, removing the double negatives.**

  a I didn't see nothing! _____

  b He never smiles at no one. _____

  c I didn't get no answer. _____

  d Steve didn't get none. _____

  e This film isn't no good. _____

Tough	OK	Got it!

0   14

Total

14

Adapting texts 2

We have already seen how **vocabulary** and **sentence structure** are altered depending on the audience. We know that different **dialect terms** and **abbreviations** are used in **informal** spoken English, but these can be very confusing for someone learning English as a foreign language. **Imagery** and **complex sentences** can also be difficult for non-native speakers to understand.

1. **Circle any terms that would be confusing for someone learning English.**

   a "Wash your donnies before dinner please!"

   b It ain't arf hot in 'ere.

   c Sheryl went barmy when Pete told her how the story ended.

   d "Gerr off! Stop larkin about!"

   e She went to see the babbee and then went for a mooch round the shops.

   f "Who's that bloke?"

2. **Rewrite this text by simplifying any imagery and complex sentences.**   *(4 marks)*

   The blanket of snow stretched as far as the eye could see, like a crisp, clean sheet on a freshly made bed. The harsh, grey circle of the M25 that snaked around the nation's capital, and which was usually so full of noise and fumes, was silent at last. Where roaring traffic normally trudged, and restless drivers regularly sat, there was nothing but a peaceful expanse of white. The icy carpet would soon thaw, warmed by the burning ball of fire in the sky, but for now it was a wonderful sight to behold.

   _____

   _____

   _____

   _____

   _____

   _____

0			10
Tough	OK	Got it!	

Total

/10

Prepositions

> A **preposition** links **nouns**, **pronouns** and **phrases** to other words in a sentence.
>
> **Pre** means **before** or in front of, so a **preposition** is placed **in front** of a noun.
>
> Prepositions tell you where the noun is:
> - in time   She ate her sandwich **before** class.
> - in place   The aeroplane is **above** the clouds.

1. Underline the prepositions in this group of words.   *(14 marks, ½ mark for each)*

about   past   sometimes   against   onto   among   at   behind

beside   soon   between   under   now   but   by   down   during

upon   for   from   into   like   near   of   off   out

underneath   over   loudly   since   through   towards throughout

2. Underline the nouns and pronouns and circle the prepositions.

a Before I go out I want to finish this picture.

b Jack climbed up the beanstalk to the very top.

c We walked along the winding path to the river.

d The dog went wild and chased the rabbit across the common.

e The earth travels around the sun once a day.

3. Complete these sentences with the most appropriate prepositions.

at   beyond   to   with   above   on   in   below

a We went to the fair _____ the common yesterday.

b _____ the front of this book, _____ the title, is the author's name.

c Gran agreed _____ Mum that I was very similar _____ looks _____ Dad.

d To do that is really _____ and _____ the call of duty!

0			23
Tough	OK	Got it!	

Total

23 / 23

53

Clauses

> **Subordinate clauses** usually begin with a **connective** such as:
>
> until   even though   although   since   after   while   because   as
>
> **Although** I would like to go out, it's raining too heavily.
>
> Subordinate clauses must always be connected to, or embedded in, a main clause to make sense.

1. **Underline the subordinate clauses in these sentences and write the main clauses.**

   a While Mum was driving, I noticed that the leaves had begun to change colour.

   _____

   b Every Saturday, because I want to learn a new language, I go to Spanish class.

   _____

   c My language skills, while they are getting better every day, could be even better.

   _____

   d After I got home from school, I completed my homework before watching TV.

   _____

2. **Make full sentences using the conjunctions, subordinate and main clauses.**

Conjunctions	Subordinate Clauses	Main Clauses
until	we didn't have much	they had a cup of coffee
even though	I have time	I can't give you a mark
when	they had finished shopping	we shared our food
after	you hand in your homework	I like reading stories

   a _____

   b _____

   c _____

   d _____

			Total
0 Tough	OK	Got it! 8	8

Punctuating sentences

> Remember:
> A **subordinate clause** is separated from a **main clause** by a **comma**.
>   With Mum and Dad each carrying a suitcase, we set off for the station.
>
> If it is embedded in a main clause it has a comma at either end:
>   Tomorrow, if it's fine, we will go on the rollercoaster.

1. **Put commas in these sentences to separate the clauses.**

   a Bev if you take too long to get dressed you'll be late for school.

   b When the whistle blew everyone sprinted down the track.

   c If it doesn't rain this afternoon we'll go to the park.

   d I turned away after hugging Mum tightly and got on the bus.

   e If I can I'll come and visit you.

   f Trisha who was 10 helped Michael up the stairs.

> Remember:
> For direct speech, speech marks are needed.
>   "Let's go to see Fred," suggested Kamal.

2. **Write these sentences using correct punctuation.**

   a tomorrow bright and early we leave for florida

   _____

   b how long will you be asked mum its time we were off

   _____

   c shes gone now thought sarah but for how long

   _____

   d needless to say with all the excitement she forgot her promise

   _____

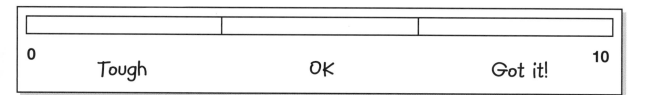

| 0 | | | 10 |
| Tough | OK | Got it! | |

Total

/10

Apostrophes

Apostrophes can be used to show possession; that something belongs to someone.

- For nouns that **do not end in s**, write **'s** after the noun.
  the girl**'s** doll   the doll belongs to one **girl**

- For nouns that **ends in s**, just add **'** to the noun.
  the girls**'** doll   the doll belongs to some **girls**

- When two or more nouns are involved, write **'s** after the last noun.
  Lucy and Abby**'s** doll.   the doll belongs to Lucy and Abby

1. **Write these phrases, including the apostrophes.**

   a the boys ruler _____   **b** three boys rulers _____

   c the dogs bone _____   **d** two dogs bones _____

   e the squirrels tail _____   **f** five squirrels tails _____

   g the bus wheels _____   **h** four buses wheels _____

2. **Now write these phrases and include the apostrophes.**

   a the persons food _____   **b** the peoples food _____

   c the mans team _____   **d** the mens team _____

   e the womans clothes _____   **f** the womens clothes _____

   g the childs toys _____   **h** the childrens toys _____

3. **Rewrite these sentences using apostrophes to show possession.**

   a We went in the car of Uncle Mike. _We went in Uncle Mike's car._____

   b She borrowed the cardigan off Tina. _____

   c We stroked the dog belonging to Raul and Natalia. _____

   d Jerry opened the cage of the budgie. _____

   e We went to the house of Toby. _____

| 0 | Tough | OK | Got it! | 20 |

Total

/20

> **Comments** and **phrases** can be separated from sentences with different types of punctuation.
> **Single dashes attach** extra comments to a sentence:
>   It was locked – wasn't it?
> and **introduce** further explanation:
>   She won't be in – she is ill with flu.

1. Add dashes where appropriate in these sentences.

  a I looked inside the cage for Polly she wasn't there!

  b Come at 2 I'll be ready.

  c Stay a little longer you know you want to.

  d The door creaked open slowly what lay inside?

> **Pairs** of **dashes separate** additional information and draw attention to it:
>   My last car – a large saloon – regularly broke down.
> The sentence must still make sense if what's between the dashes is deleted:
>   My last car regularly broke down.

2. Add pairs of dashes to draw attention to the additional information.

  a Inside the parcel was a scarf a soft red one from Auntie Jo.

  b She unwrapped the chocolate the only one left and put it in her mouth.

  c No one not even Ben was strong enough to lift the bench.

  d There were two people Akash and Stuart in front of me in the dinner queue.

> **Brackets enclose** useful but non-essential information:
>   We are going on holiday **(**weather permitting**)** in August.
>   Roald Dahl **(**1916–1990**)** wrote *The BFG*.

3. Use brackets to enclose the additional information in these sentences.

  a Jacqueline Wilson author of several books is coming to our town tomorrow.

  b The A380 an aeroplane is as long as a football pitch.

  c His new car a VW Golf was a lovely ocean green colour.

  d I didn't see him do it I was looking the other way at the time but I know it was him.

0			12
Tough	OK	Got it!	

Total

/12

All around the world people tell stories, but they tell them in different ways.

Here is the start of a story from Scotland. Read the first part.

Once, a long time ago, there was a gentleman who had two lassies. The oldest was ugly and ill natured, but the youngest was a bonnie lassie and good; but the ugly one was the favourite with her father and mother. So they ill used the youngest in every way, and they sent her into the woods to herd cattle. Well, amongst the cattle was a red calf, and one day it said to the lassie, "Come wi' me." So the lassie followed the calf through the wood, and they came to a bonnie hoosie, where there was a nice dinner ready for them; and after they had feasted on everything nice they went back to the herding.

1. **What kind of story do you think this will be? Why?**

   _____

   _____

2. **What is unusual about the way the story is written?**

   _____

3. **What do you think these words mean?**

   a lassie _____

   b bonnie hoosie _____

   c ill used _____

Here is the next part of the story. The older sister decides to kill the girl, so the calf and the girl run away.

And they set off again and travelled, and travelled, till they came to the king's house. They went in, and asked if they wanted a servant. The mistress said she wanted a kitchen lassie, and she would take Rashin-Coatie. So the lassie and the calf stoppit in the king's house, and everybody was well pleased with her; and when Yule came, they said she was to stop at home and make the dinner, while all the rest went to the kirk. After they were away the calf asked if she would like to go. She said she would, but she had no clothes, and she could not leave the dinner. The calf said he would give her clothes, and make the dinner too. He went out, and came back with a grand dress, all silk and satin, and such a nice pair of slippers.

So she went to the kirk, and nobody kent it was Rashin-Coatie. They wondered who the bonnie lady could be; and, as soon as the young prince saw her, he fell in love with her. Rashin-Coatie left before the rest, so that she might get home in time to take off her dress, and look after the dinner. When the prince saw her leaving, he made for the door to stop her; but she jumped past him, and in the hurry lost one of her shoes. The prince kept the shoe, and Rashin-Coatie got home all right, and the folk said the dinner was very nice.

4. **Who do you think Rashin-Coatie is? Circle the right answer.**

   the calf   the lassie   someone else

5. **What time of year is the story set in?**

   _____

6. **What do you think these words mean?**

   a stoppit _____

   b kent _____

   c kirk _____

7. **What famous story does this remind you of?**

   _____

8. **What differences can you notice between Rashin-Coatie and the other famous story? Note down at least four differences.** *(4 marks)*

Rashin-Coatie	Other Story

Objective or subjective?

Non-fiction texts may be **objective** or **subjective**.

- **Subjective texts** are written from a particular point of view. They are often **biased** – they aim to persuade the reader to believe or do something. **Advertisements** are subjective texts.

- **Objective texts** aim to give facts, without any bias.

1. **Read these texts then answer the questions.**

Text A

The council has put forward a proposal for a new road. It will link two motorways and is expected to ease traffic in the city. In order to construct the road, the compulsory purchase of some properties will be necessary and certain local roads will need to be rerouted. Many local jobs will be created by the development.

Text B

YOUR council is trying to force a new road upon YOU, which it says will take traffic away from the city – but at what cost? Hundreds of homeowners will lose their properties! Whole villages will be destroyed by the developers' demolition ball! Countless fields of fertile farmland will be coated in concrete! And what of the ancient roadways? Are you expected to just sit back and watch them be destroyed?

Surely the council must be deluded if it really thinks this new road will keep traffic away from the city? The real truth is that building more roads only increases traffic. And with more roads, comes more heavy industry. Do we really want all that noise and pollution defiling our beautiful countryside? Homes will be bulldozed, jobs lost and ways of life that are thousands of years old will be destroyed!

STOP this madness in its tracks – VOTE NO TO THE ROAD!

---

1. **Which text appears to be objective and which text appears to be subjective?**

_____

_____

2. **What key detail, which has been excluded from Text B, is included in Text A? Why do you think it has been omitted from Text B?**

_____

_____

3. **What four-word phrase disguises opinion as fact in Text B?**

_____

4. **Circle all the powerful verbs and underline the rhetorical questions in Text B.**

$\left(10\ marks,\ verbs:\ \frac{1}{2}\ mark\ for\ each\right)$

5. **Which two adjectives in Text B indicate exaggeration?**

_____

6. **Write down all the examples of alliteration used in Text B.**   *(4 marks)*

_____

_____

7. **Why has the writer of Text B used capital letters for some words?**

_____

_____

8. **Who do you think could have written each text? Explain your answer.**

_____

_____

_____

9. **Do you think either text presents a complete picture? Explain your answer.**

_____

_____

_____

0	Tough	OK	Got it!	21

Total

/21

61

How am I doing?

1. **Use an antonym of each word in brackets to complete these sentences.**

    a He always was a very _____ boy. (naughty)

    b It was an incredibly _____ game to win. (easy)

    c That holiday will be really _____. (cheap)

    d Our new home is very _____ the old one. (far)

2. **Rewrite these words correctly, putting in the missing unstressed vowels.**

    a voluntry _____

    b frightning _____

    c mystry _____

    d diffrence _____

    e listning _____

    f categry _____

    g genrous _____

    h diry _____

3. **Complete these words with the correct ie or ei letter string.**

    a sc_____nce   **b** glac_____r   **c** anc_____nt   **d** w_____rd

    e _____ghth   **f** t_____   **g** _____ther   **h** handkerch_____f

4. **Add the correct prefix in, im, il or ir to these words.**

    a _____plant   **b** _____correct   **c** _____definite   **d** _____visible

    e ___rational   **f** _____legible   **g** _____licit   **h** _____balance

5. **Complete the sentences. The region each word comes from is in brackets.**

    giraffe   canoe   anorak   kindergarten

    a I wear my _____ in the cold, wet weather. (North America)

    b They paddled the _____ down the river. (Caribbean)

    c The tallest living animal is the _____ . (Arabia)

    d _____ is another name for a nursery class. (Germany)

6. **Write the common abbreviation or acronym for the terms below.**

    a bed and breakfast _____   **b** hippopotamus _____   **c** aeroplane _____

    d do it yourself _____   **e** please turn over _____   **f** photograph _____

7. **Complete these sentences using conjunctions.**

   a I could have bought the CD _____ I decided to save my money instead.

   b Would you like to go swimming _____ would you rather go bowling?

   c I was very upset _____ my mum gave me a hug.

8. **Rewrite these sentences correctly, removing the double negatives.**

   a Nobody's never seen it! _____

   b We aren't going no more. _____

   c I haven't never done that. _____

9. **Circle the prepositions in these sentences.**

   a The vacuum cleaner is under the stairs, near the mop and bucket.

   b I put the book down beside my drink and walked across the room to the door.

   c He walked along the road and through the woods towards the river.

10. **Underline the subordinate clauses in these sentences.**

    a I asked Mum, when she came off the phone, if I could go to Ranjit's house.

    b Although it was nearly dinner time, we went to the park.

    c After we had seen Granny, Mum took us shopping for the afternoon.

11. **Rewrite these sentences, changing all nouns to plurals and using apostrophes to show possession.**

    a The coat belonging to the man. _____

    b The glass belonging to the girl. _____

    c The tail belonging to the dog. _____

12. **Write in the missing commas, colons, semicolons, dashes and brackets.**

    a Charles Dickens 1812–1870 wrote many fine novels.

    b He looked up slowly what was it?

    c He bought a bunch of bananas a punnet of raspberries and two plums for dessert.

Total

56

63

Try the 10–11 years book

Unstressed vowels

> **Unstressed vowels** are either:
> • not sounded clearly, for example the second 'a' in parallel (it sounds like 'uh')
> OR
> • not sounded at all, for example the 'e' in geography.

QUICK TIP!
Use a dictionary to look up any spellings you are unsure about.

1. **Say these words and underline the unstressed vowels.**

   a fattening **b** dandelion **c** miniature **d** interest **e** astronomy

   f abandon **g** lettuce **h** benefit **i** journalist **j** mathematics

2. **Write the unstressed vowels in these words.**

   a tel__vision **b** parli__ment **c** veg__table **d** cons__n__nt **e** cemet__ry

   f ov__n **g** sign__ture **h** med__cine **i** muscl__ **j** gramm__r

3. **These words have unstressed vowels in them. Underline the words that are spelt correctly.**

   a separate seperate **b** definate definite **c** intresting interesting

   d teluphone telephone **e** nuisance nusance **f** secrutry secretary

   g mischevus mischevious **h** temperature temprature **i** lemonade lemunade

4. **When a word ending in ary, ery or ory is spoken it can be hard to tell how to spell the ending. Write the words in the correct columns depending upon their endings.**

   (6 marks)

Words	ary endings	ery endings	ory endings
lott _ _ _ Febru _ _ _			
hist _ _ _ Janu _ _ _			
fact _ _ _ bound _ _ _			
categ _ _ _ station _ _ _			
volunt _ _ _ jewell _ _ _			
batt _ _ _ veterin _ _ _			

QUICK TIP!
One word belongs in two columns. Which word is it?

0			35
Tough	OK	Got it!	

Total

35

64

No Nonsense

Bond is the number 1 provider of 11+ practice, helping millions of children improve their literacy and numeracy skills.

Bond No Nonsense English for 9–10 years provides clear, straightforward exercises to help boost your child's confidence and ability in English. Divided into separate sections that cover each key skill, this book establishes strong foundations in core English, supporting and reinforcing school learning.

- **Structured step-by-step lessons**
  Split into three sections with a progress check between each one

- **Teaching and quick tips**
  Each lesson includes a 'How to do' explanation, supported with quick tips for extra help

- **Carefully graded practice questions**
  Designed for steady progression pitched at just the right level

- **Easy-to-remove answer section with parents' notes**
  Located in the centre of the book

Other titles available at this age group in the **Bond English** range:

 No Nonsense

 Up to Speed Papers

 Assessment Papers

 10 Minute Tests

 Stretch Papers

 Get Ready for Secondary School

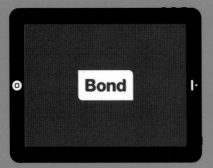

Discover more 11+ practice at

bond11plus.co.uk

10–11+	
9–10	
8–9	
7–8	

OXFORD
UNIVERSITY PRESS

www.oup.com

ISBN 978-0-19-274043-4

9 780192 740434

KS-955-008

My First

Hamster

Veronica Ross

Chrysalis Children's Books

First published in the UK in 2002 by

Chrysalis Children's Books

An imprint of Chrysalis Books Group Plc

The Chrysalis Building, Bramley Road, London W10 6SP

Paperback edition first published in 2004

Copyright © Chrysalis Books Group Plc 2002

Text by Veronica Ross

ISBN 1 84138 401 1 (hb)

ISBN 1 84458 231 0 (pb)

British Library Cataloguing in Publication Data for this book is available from the British Library.

Designer: Helen James

Picture researcher: Terry Forshaw

Consultants: Frazer Swift and Nikki Spevack

Printed in China

10 9 8 7 6 5 4 3 2 1

All photography Warren Photographic/Jane Burton with the exception of:
9 (T) FLPA/Hans Dieter Brandl, (B) & Front Cover (inset) Animal PhotographySally Anne Thompson; 11 Ardea/John Daniels; 13 Bubbles/Dr Hercules Robinson; 15 RSPCA Photolibrary/Angela Hampton; 17, 20 Animal Photography/Sally Anne Thompson; 21 Bubbles/Ian West; 25 RSPCA Photolibrary/Angela Hampton; 26 & 28 Animal Photography/Sally Anne Thompson; 29 RSPCA Photolibrary/Angela Hampton.

Contents

Your pet hamster

Hamsters are easy to tame and great fun to own, but they do need to be treated gently. You will have to look after your pet carefully and make sure that it is happy, healthy and well fed.

4

paws

ears

tail

When you go on holiday, you will have to find someone who will look after your hamster while you are away.

Young children with pets should always be supervised by an adult. Please see notes for parents on page 32.

What is a hamster?

Hamsters are small and furry with stumpy tails. They belong to a family of animals called rodents. All rodents have very sharp teeth that grow all the time. Hamsters have good hearing, but they can't see very well.

Small hamsters, like these two, are called dwarf hamsters.

This hamster has heard a noise. It is standing on its back legs and listening hard.

Hamsters with long hair need to be brushed every day.

Hamsters are very curious. They like to go exploring.

Hamster habits

Do not wake your hamster when it is asleep.

Hamsters sleep for most of the day and wake up at night. Wild hamsters search for food at night, but your pet will want to play.

Hamsters like to make a cosy nest out of their bedding.

In the wild, hamsters live
in underground burrows
with lots of tunnels.

Hamsters have pouches
in their cheeks which they
stuff with food. They store
the food to eat later.

Newborn hamsters

Hamsters are born with their eyes closed and no fur. At two weeks they have soft, furry coats.

This tiny baby hamster is drinking milk from its mother. The milk will help it grow big and strong.

Hamster babies are very small. The mother often carries them in her mouth.

Baby hamsters can walk about, but they sometimes fall over. They like to play with their brothers and sisters.

When they are six weeks old, hamsters are ready to leave their mother.

Choosing a hamster

Look for a hamster that seems lively. It should be busy scurrying around the cage.

A healthy hamster has thick, silky fur, bright eyes and a clean nose.

Spend some
time playing
with the
hamsters
before you
choose one
you like.

Both males and females make
good pets, but do not keep more
than one hamster in a cage.

Buy your hamster from a pet shop or
from a hamster breeder. An animal
shelter may have hamsters too.

A place to live

Hamsters can live in
a cage or a tank. The tank
in the picture has lots of rooms. It is
like a burrow where wild hamsters live.

Put paper
bedding or
hay into the
nesting box.

Your pet will love running through the tunnels in this tank.

Put a deep layer of sawdust or wood shavings in the bottom of the cage or tank for your pet to dig in.

Keep your pet's home indoors. Don't put it in a draught, in bright sunlight or near a radiator.

Handling your hamster

Give your pet time to
settle into its new home
before you pick it up.
Stroke it gently and
give it some food.

Hold your
hamster close
to your body so
that it feels safe.

Take care if you
hold your finger
out to your pet.
It might think it's
food and bite you!

Sit down or kneel on the floor. Turn to
face your pet so that it can see you
and lift it up with both hands.

If your pet falls and you
think that it is hurt, take
it to the vet at once.

Feeding your hamster

In the morning feed your pet fresh fruit and vegetables. In the evening, give it a bowl of special hamster food from a pet shop.

Hamsters like to gnaw hard vegetables.

Give your pet fresh
water every day. Put
it in a drip feed bottle.

Hamsters enjoy carrots,
apples, pears, grapes
and tomatoes.

Do not give your
pet too much food.

Clean and tidy

Hamsters are very good at keeping clean. They lick their paws and use them to wash themselves all over.

This hamster is using its claws to comb its fur.

Hold your pet gently and smell its fur. A healthy hamster should smell clean all over.

If you have a long-haired hamster you can brush it gently with a clean toothbrush.

You can help your pet keep tidy by gently untangling knots in its fur with your fingers.

Play time

Give your pet an exercise wheel to play on. Make sure that there are no gaps in it where it could trap its leg.

At night, a hamster can run for several kilometres on an exercise wheel.

This hamster is having fun in its toy house.

Hamsters like toys to play with. Put a cardboard tube or half a coconut shell in its cage for it to explore.

If you let your hamster out of its cage, make sure you keep the doors and windows closed.

A clean home

Remove old food and droppings from your pet's home once a day and wash the food bowl. Clean the water bottle once a week.

Once a month clean the cage or tank with soapy water and special disinfectant.

Put in new bedding once a week, but don't throw out all the old bedding.

Sweep up the wood shavings or sawdust and put in a fresh layer once a week.

When you clean your pet's home, wear gloves or wash your hands with soap and water afterwards.

Staying healthy

If your hamster has a clean home and the right food to eat, it should stay fit and healthy.

Don't let your hamster play with another hamster – they may fight.

A healthy hamster can live for up to three years.

Your hamster needs lots of exercise to stay healthy. Play with your pet at least once a day.

As your pet gets older it might lose its fur and put on weight. Take care not to feed it too much.

Visiting the vet

You will be able
to tell if your hamster
isn't feeling well. If it has
runny eyes or nose, or if its fur looks
dull you may need to take it to the vet.

Take your hamster
to see the vet once a
year for a check-up.

Your pet's teeth should be short and sharp.

If your pet's teeth grow too long your vet can cut and file them down.

Check your pet every day. If you think it seems unwell, take it to the vet.

Words to remember

animal shelter A home for unwanted pets.

bedding Soft hay or shredded paper from a pet shop.

breeder A person who sells animals.

burrow Where wild hamsters live.

file To smooth down.

gnaw To chew.

groom To brush and comb an animal's fur.

pouches Spaces in a hamster's cheeks where it can store food.

rodent The name of a group of animals. Rodents have very sharp front teeth. Rats, mice and squirrels are also rodents.

scurrying Moving quickly.

tank A glass or plastic container in which hamsters live.

vet An animal doctor.

Index

Notes for parents

If you decide to buy a hamster for your child, it will be your responsibility to ensure that the animal is healthy, happy and safe. You will need to make sure that your child handles the hamster correctly and does not harm it. Here are some points you should bear in mind before you buy a hamster:

- Hamsters should be six weeks old before they leave their mother.

- Hamsters sleep for most of the day and are active at night. They can be very noisy at a time when the rest of the household wants to go to sleep. If this is going to be irritating, rabbits or guinea pigs might be a better choice.

- A hamster cage or tank must be kept indoors. If your pet gets too cold, it may die.

- Do you know someone who will look after your hamster when you go on holiday?

- Hamsters should be kept on their own. If you keep more than one hamster in a cage they will fight.

- If you have any questions about looking after your hamster, contact your local vet.